Fifth Edition

YOUR VOICE
AT ITS BEST

Fifth Edition

YOUR VOICE AT ITS BEST

enhancement of the healthy voice, help for the troubled voice

David Blair McClosky
with members of the McClosky Institute of Voice

WAVELAND
PRESS, INC.
Long Grove, Illinois

For information about this book, contact:
 Waveland Press, Inc.
 4180 IL Route 83, Suite 101
 Long Grove, IL 60047-9580
 (847) 634-0081
 info@waveland.com
 www.waveland.com

McClosky Institute of Voice
www.mcclosky.org

Copyright © 2011 by McClosky Institute of Voice
Numerous editions of this work have appeared since its original publication
in 1959. This Fifth Edition has been made possible through special arrange-
ment with Boston Music Company, a division of Music Sales Corporation.

10-digit ISBN 1-57766-705-0
13-digit ISBN 978-1-57766-705-6

Printed in the United States of America

7 6 5 4 3 2 1

Contents

Foreword

Jay D. Lane, CMVT, PhD

$\mathcal{D}$avid Blair McClosky was a pioneer in physiologically-based voice teaching. For years he taught, performed, studied the vocal mechanism, and worked with doctors and their patients to rehabilitate damaged voices. He had already learned a great deal about the human voice when, in 1946, a crisis propelled him to synthesize all he knew into what we now call "the McClosky Technique."

McClosky wrote two books, *Your Voice at its Best* (1959, revised 1978) and *Voice in Song and Speech* (1984, with Barbara McClosky), in which he put forth his method for the healthy production of the human voice. These two books have been combined into one in the present volume. Some material has been updated and expanded, especially with regard to scientific and medical concerns, but the fundamental technique remains just as McClosky developed it.

The McClosky method itself is beautifully simple and easy to comprehend. Its goal is functional efficiency: coordinating the different parts of the vocal mechanism so that, whether in song or speech, each part of the body is doing its proper job, with little or no effort wasted. With time and diligent practice, the entire body becomes a musical instrument.

Because the McClosky approach deals with all the underlying issues of voice production, it requires careful work. This method builds the voice "from the foundation up." It may seem slow at first, but with a good will and a few months of regular practice, the foundations are built for healthy singing and speaking for a lifetime.

Introduction

(1959 Edition)

David Blair McClosky

The art of speaking and the closely related art of singing have been practiced for thousands of years and have remained arts. There is no doubt but that man, ever since he first found he could make sounds, has tried to enlarge the possibilities of phonation and enhance the sounds he produced. But in recent years, not much more than a hundred to be exact, a modicum of science has slowly found its way into the art of producing vocal sound, or phonation. Only at this comparatively late date in forensic, dramatic, and musical history are we beginning to understand some of the fundamentals on which a sound and lasting ability to speak and sing can be established.

Some temerity is required for anyone to offer even an approach to a better method of phonation. No book can possibly take the place of a good teacher. It would be pretentious indeed to assume that any teacher is qualified as yet to set up a completely new theory of voice production. Nevertheless, in the past few years, with the aid of new techniques and apparatus in related fields, a few things have been learned which can make a meaningful contribution to the body of knowledge which others have accumulated.

To have authority, suggestions for improving the voice should be based on seasoned observation, analysis, and application, not alone by an experienced singer or speaker, but by a teacher who has seen hundreds of his students practice successfully the principles he expounds. The approach offered here is the result of more than twenty-seven years of study, speaking, singing, teaching of students and teachers, and therapeutic work with medical scientists specializing in treatment of the throat and larynx. The studio has been my laboratory, and my "guinea pigs" have been singers and speakers, young and old, beginners and veterans.

What are these principles?

First, let me tell you for what purposes this guide has been written and for what groups of persons it has been designed.

My purpose is to provide a simple and clear explanation of the processes involved in correct and therefore healthy and long-lasting vocal-sound production, and how they may be applied by teachers, students, ministers, public speakers and businessmen, as well as by other mature and professional speakers and singers. I include also those who are developing their voices and those who have misused them and need vocal rehabilitation.

Possibly what I have to offer can be most useful to teachers of singing; many of them, I have found, are excellent and thorough musicians, doing a fine job of instruction in expression, interpretation and the coaching of song literature, but actually deficient in their knowledge of the physical facts connected with the singing mechanism. They know what they want to hear in a voice but are not sufficiently schooled in the fundamentals of vocal function. These teachers, I realize, will be slow to adopt any new approach differing from their present method, but I trust will be open-minded enough to weigh my observations with such care as they may merit.

Teachers of speech, I have found, are inclined to differentiate sharply between their own art and the teaching of singing. They seem to be more detached in their approach than singing teachers; their objectives are more tangible and their methods can be more practical. They sometimes disparage what appears to them to be the somewhat haphazard methods of singing teachers. Nevertheless, correct sound production applies quite as much to the teaching of speech as to the teaching of singing, and there is enough in common between the two to warrant any speech teacher's assimilation of much that I have to submit. Obviously both singing and speaking are produced by the same set of vocal cords, even though they may be motivated by different areas in the brain. It is still true that "well spoken is half sung," and I might add conversely that "singing is speech on pitch."

Even those teachers who do not accept all my principles will find that students who have read this book will have less to *unlearn* and will be more responsive to whatever helpful instruction they are offered than those students who have not been exposed to these preparatory fundamentals.

If you are a student of speech or of singing, I will say to you that this book is no substitute for a good teacher. There is and can be no satisfactory alternative to the personal observation, encouragement, and guidance of a knowledgeable instructor. This is a "do-it-yourself "guide only insofar as it will *prepare you to be a better student*. As any honest teacher prefers to work with well-prepared students, so any aspiring student will get more out of his or her instruction when the preliminaries have been understood in advance. These preliminaries need not be tedious and can be fascinating. And, if correctly established, they are one part of the learning program that teachers will prefer to find already accomplished.

It is easy to spoil a good natural voice and there are millions of voices that have been damaged—if very few beyond repair—by faulty training. Any student who reads this will do well to ask himself: "Could my adoption of this approach possibly harm me?" As you read on, your common sense will tell you that proper relaxation of the muscles surrounding the vocal apparatus never harmed anyone and that the other steps described are all in the direction of harmless and constructive progress. You cannot possibly *lose* anything, and I can promise you without qualification that if you will read this message thoughtfully and make even a slight effort to put these principles to test and into practice, you will have assisted any teacher of voice or speech to make more rapid and substantial progress with the development of your voice.

In addition to what this book can do for students and teachers, I feel warranted in believing that it can also be of help to throat specialists. For twenty-seven years, I have worked with several otolaryngologists in the therapeutic correction of vocal disorders. Through their interest, guidance, and collaboration I have conducted seminars and lectured before their gatherings and have treated hundreds of cases involving functional and psychological disorders affecting the larynx. One of the things I respect most about the medical profession is that its members never consider that they have arrived at the *ultimate* understanding of the disorders they treat, or feel that there is nothing more for them to learn. Without their interest and help, I would never have incentive or the confidence to work steadily toward surer methods and techniques for improving and rehabilitating the voice.

If you are a singer or a speaker whose voice has deteriorated or is failing, I can say to you with confidence that the unreclaimable voice is rare. With the proper training in the sort of techniques outlined in this book, your voice should not only return to normal but improve and develop. The many faults and bad habits resulting from poor training can usually be remedied easily, and few indeed are justified in despairing.

The human voice is an instrument capable of producing the most astonishing range of sounds, colors, emotions, and musical tones. It was not intended by nature to make music, or even speech, but has evolved and developed to these capabilities. We have to understand this instrument, its possibilities, limitations, and the techniques of using it, quite as clearly as we need to comprehend the workings of a piano, a violin, or a clarinet. Because the working of our own instrument is invisible—except as modern science by means of X-ray and slow-motion pictures has visualized it—its functions have until recently been fairly obscure. Therefore, it is not so easy to understand as a man-made instrument that we can look at, touch, and examine minutely. The need for understanding is no less, however. The more we know about the human voice and how it functions, the better we shall be able to use it to its fullest as a means of expression.

Every doctor depends on the study of illness, or what he calls *pathology*, to learn more about health. *Therapeutics*, the curative treatment of disease, is facilitated by first knowing exactly what is wrong. So, in singing and speaking, I first came to a clear realization of what I had learned about correct vocalization when, in 1946, 1 had to cure myself on short notice of a vocal weakness that had developed following a long period of illness and convalescence in an Army hospital at Spokane. (I had contracted a severe chest ailment following my transfer from the tropics to a cold climate while in my last year with the Army Air Force during World War II.) I was scheduled to give a song recital at Town Hall in New York City during my first year as a member of the voice faculty at Syracuse University's College of Music. As my rehearsals for this concert went on, I became increasingly aware of the fact that my throat was not in a healthy condition. Apparently I had attempted to resume my singing career too soon following the aforementioned illness, which had confined me for almost a year. My throat specialist, the late Dr. Irl Blaisdell, told me to cancel the recital, as it would be impossible to correct the condition in the fortnight remaining. By this time, however, it was too late to postpone the performance. Then came the supreme test of what I had learned about relaxation, breathing, support, coordination, and resonance. During those two weeks, I called upon all the knowledge I had of the workings of the voice and put the time that would have ordinarily been spent in rehearsing the recital songs toward light vocal exercises. By the time the recital took place, Dr. Blaisdell declared my larynx to be in normal condition and I was able to proceed with complete confidence. This crisis became a turning point in my, life, vocally speaking, leading from there to new developments in vocal therapeutics. What had been only theory had now been tested and proven on my own person in an emergency. From that day to this I have never doubted the efficacy of the curative method I then employed and which I have since developed and practiced for twelve years but which until now, I was not ready to publish.

From the many physicians with whom I have worked I have learned caution, patience, and humility. Therefore I do not offer *Your Voice at Its Best* as the last word on the subject. Disorders caused by faulty use of the voice, such as chronic laryngitis, vocal nodules and polyps, bowed vocal cords, contact ulcers, use of false cords in phonation, have, time after time, been completely cured. Other pathological conditions, such as hysterical dysphonia and aphonia, retarded adolescent or falsetto voice, some forms of paralysis such as might result from a thyroidectomy in which the recurrent laryngeal nerve has been damaged, or laryngo-fissure (in which a vocal cord has been removed) have been cured or definitely helped. However, many more case histories must be added to the substantial number already recorded before I shall feel that I have made a conclusive and lasting contribution to voice therapy.

I am not so modest about what I have learned about the teaching of singing and speaking from my experience and quarter-century of therapeutic practice. *A method that is effective in reclaiming impaired voices must have exceptional merit in maintaining the health of unimpaired ones and allowing them to develop under the best possible conditions.*

Chapter 1

The McClosky Technique

Posture and Breathing

The Structures of Breathing

"As natural as breathing" is proverbial, but to the speaker and singer there is a lot more to it than that. Relaxation clears the track for vocalizing, but *breath* is the motive power. Without a clear understanding of how to improve on natural respiration, no singer or speaker can be assured of maintaining the needed relaxation, the effortless emission of sound, or vocal health.

Breathing is one of the few bodily functions that is both unconscious and conscious, involuntary and, within well-defined limits, voluntary. After running or a steep climb, we are conscious of being out of breath. But, generally speaking, we give little thought to breath control. In singing and speaking, however, we have to pay a great deal of attention to it until, through careful thought and with helpful exercises, correct breathing for phonation becomes as automatic as driving a car. When we are not speaking or singing or thinking about breathing, enough air passes into our lungs without effort to provide the necessary exchange of oxygen for carbon dioxide. As we breathe, the rhythmic action, controlled by the respiratory center of the brain, goes on quietly and uninterruptedly.

As soon as we open our mouths to sing or speak, however, a different kind of breathing should begin. Our conscious mind is brought into play. We must have enough breath to get through a sentence or a musical phrase without either hesitation or gulping, and perhaps keep this up for hours at a time. Furthermore, we must have enough breath and breath control to sustain and even amplify our voice while completing a phrase. If we are performing professionally, we must be able to keep on phonating for a long period of time while retaining a fresh, clear, and steady voice. This will not be possible if we

1

are constantly gasping for breath or discovering, in the middle of a phrase, that we are "out of gas." Therefore, we must know the components of our breathing apparatus and how to use them. Just as we learn to hold a golf club and perfect our swing to send the ball down the fairway, so must we learn to coordinate the use of all of our breathing muscles.

When we breathe for phonation we take a larger volume of air than for passive breathing, and it no longer flows in and out rhythmically, since we exhale much more slowly than we inhale. One of the chief aims in learning to breathe consciously is to replenish our breath quickly and effortlessly without disturbing the flow of our spoken or musical meaning and then to propel our breath gradually and under complete but relaxed control, and to finish each phrase in the most telling manner. Breath pressure will, of course, vary greatly according to the volume and quality of sound produced.

Aside from its helpful and necessary effect on producing sound, the full development of breathing power contributes to general health and well-being. Deep breathing has long been recognized as one of the most salutary physical habits. The extra oxygen taken in with a deep breath purifies the blood and gives us extra energy. Many people go through life without ever taking a really deep breath except when strenuous exercise forces them to do so. Every athlete knows that the capacity to perform at optimum level depends in large part on the ability to supply oneself with the needed extra oxygen.

Our breathing apparatus consists of the lungs, with their surrounding rib cage, and the passages that carry air to the mouth and nose, consisting of the bronchi, the trachea or windpipe, the larynx, and the pharynx; the diaphragm; and abdominal muscles (see appendix A, figures 1–3).

The rib cage is flexible. It consists of twelve pairs of ribs jointed to the spine in back and connected to the sternum (breastbone) in front by cartilage, except for the two floating ribs at the bottom, which are joined to the abdominal wall by bands of connective tissue. The muscles inside and between the ribs are called *intercostals;* the name indicates the functions of these muscles, since *costa* is Latin for rib. These muscles raise and lower the ribs (see appendix A, figure 2). Shallow breathing is confined to the chest and makes little use of the more powerful abdominal muscles. But it is the abdominal muscles that speakers and singers need to develop (see appendix A, figure 3).

The *diaphragm* is the most important single factor in breathing. This partition, which separates our chest or thorax from our abdomen, consists of muscle fibers that come together to a tendon at the center. It is attached all the way around at the level of the lowest complete ribs. When at rest, it has the shape of an inverted bowl under the rib cage (see appendix A, figure 4). Although elastic, the diaphragm is very powerful. When we inhale, it flattens downward, expanding the thoracic cavity, creating a partial vacuum, and drawing air into the lungs.

Although the diaphragmatic action is up and down, flattening down for inhalation and gradually returning to its dome shape during exhalation, we do not see its action. What we observe is the effect on the walls of the abdomen as the abdominal organs (viscera) are displaced (see appendix A, figure 5). The abdomen extends and retracts in coordination with the diaphragm. As we exhale, the abdominal muscles activate, firming and supporting the viscera as the diaphragm gradually relaxes back up to its normal place under the ribs. The most important aspect to good breath management is to control the rate at which the diaphragm retracts. The goal is to prevent loss of air too quickly and to sustain the airflow for phonation.

In order to accomplish this completely, another set of muscles must come into play. These are the intercostal muscles, which are attached to each of the ribs (see appendix A, figure 2). When activated, they expand the rib cage and keep the ribs from collapsing, thus helping the diaphragm to slow its return (see appendix A, figure 6). Without the help of these intercostal muscles, the lungs would lose air too quickly. There is a balance of the activation of the intercostal muscles with the contraction of the abdominal muscles. Each counterbalances the other, allowing the fine control of the breath stream, which is necessary for nuanced, sustained phonation.

Proper posture is the first answer to proper functioning of the voice and breath control. As Francesco Lamperti said "You do not sing yourself—your body sings you".

The posture about to be discussed will *allow* your body to function at its best for singing.

Posture

In order to achieve proper breathing for phonation, you must first have a good sense of alignment. Good posture can be maintained while sitting, standing, or moving.

Begin by finding good standing posture (see appendix A, figure 7):

1. Stand with feet shoulder-width apart, one foot slightly in front of the other. This makes it easy to balance the body; if the feet are too close together, one must constantly adjust one's balance. Allow the body to lean slightly toward the balls of the feet.

2. Unlock the knees; they should be neither bent nor locked.

3. Tuck the hips under. The pelvis should be rotated so that the buttocks feel slightly lower and the spine extended, with slightly less curve in the lower back. This action will help to both lengthen the lumbar spine and gently stretch the muscles of the lower back. You may feel an expansion of the lower ribs in back and a firming of the pelvic muscles. This should be done without changing the position of the upper body.

Notice that your entire spine is now more aligned, bringing your rib cage and sternum to a more upright and open position. The feeling is of spinal lengthening, both upward and downward, resulting in an open rib cage and poised position. Your shoulder structure is suspended over your ribs, neither rolled forward nor pulled back. Your head is balanced on the top of your spine and should feel almost weightless. The balance point is approximately between the ears. One-half of your skull balances in front of your A-O Joint, and the other half balances behind (see appendix A, figure 13).

To achieve ideal openness of your rib cage, stretch your arms overhead, then allow them to drop, maintaining the stretch of your upper body. You should now feel as though your spine is lengthened, your knees unlocked, your rib cage expanded, and your head balanced.

Another helpful exercise is to lie on the floor (not on a soft surface such as a mattress or a sofa), on your back with your knees bent and your feet flat on the floor. You may wish to have a book under your head, so that your neck is not curved back nor is your chin pushing down toward your chest. Your back will automatically be in approximately the alignment you want while standing. Relax for a few moments. Note how easily the action of the breath is felt in the abdomen.

Many times we find ourselves needing to sing or speak in a sitting posture. If that is the case, then be sure to maintain the spinal alignment from the hips up (see appendix A, figure 8).

If you are in an acting situation where you need to be in an odd position for some part of the staging, try to maintain your spinal alignment and rib expansion as well as you can. This may not always be easy, but if you do so, it will help you to give your best vocal performance.

Breathing

Stand with good posture as previously described. Then, allow the breath to come in through your nose with your mouth slightly open. Keeping your ribs comfortably suspended, place one hand on your abdomen and the other on your chest. If your posture has been maintained, you should feel the front and sides of your abdominal wall expand, with no action of the ribs, which, as you recall, you have been maintaining in an open position. Remember to concentrate on your complete posture. In the final analysis, no conscious action should cause the breath to enter or leave the body. This becomes an automatic action, the amount of breath being used entirely determined by the length of the spoken or sung phrase and its dynamics. Your conscious effort must for a long time be directed toward your posture or position of your body. Your breath will enter your body easily and leave it in the same way.

As you breathe, you should feel the hand on the abdomen moving (looking in a mirror as you do this may be helpful). Inhale again, and this time phonate—just make any easy sound, for example a breathy sigh, while you maintain awareness of the breath movement. Remember: as you sing, speak, or use your breath vigorously, *any movement in your body should be entirely below the rib cage*. The abdomen should always feel strong but flexible. Allowing the ribs to collapse will mean losing control of the fine balance between the abdominal and intercostal muscles.

Chapter 2

Freeing the Voice through the McClosky "Six Areas of Relaxation"

*I*n a vein similar to the Alexander Technique and the Feldenkrais Method, the McClosky Technique takes a hands-on bodywork approach to achieving vocal freedom. Performing musicians, speakers, and teachers around the world have used this technique to maintain healthy, resilient voices, even under demanding conditions. The McClosky Technique specifically focuses on the muscle groups surrounding the vocal mechanism, identifying tensions and providing a process to release those tensions over time. The McClosky Technique also emphasizes postural alignment, along with efficient, easy breathing. The task for the singer or the speaker is to build new muscle memory integrating alignment, breathing, support, and phonation, free of the extraneous muscular tensions that can impair vocal freedom. This chapter introduces and explains six areas of relaxation and how these basic tools can be applied for healthy voice use.

Proper relaxation is the first step toward achieving a truly well-coordinated voice. It is the key to all that follows. Until you are able to relax the muscles in your face, tongue, jaw, throat, and neck—all of which can interfere with the muscles controlling the vocal folds themselves—your singing and speaking will be, literally, "muscle-bound."

Every biological function involving the use of muscles relies on a balance between tension and relaxation. Most of us, in using our voices, are beset by undue muscular tightness throughout the vocal mechanism—in the throat, jaw, neck, and tongue. Unfortunately these tensions are not confined to the areas where they are needed as part of the natural muscular action

involved in the activation of the vocal folds. In fact, they are apt to predomi-
nate in the very areas where we would desire the greatest relaxation and
looseness. Instead of opening the door and allowing the caged bird—our
voice—its freedom, we constrict it with all sorts of fetters. Because achieving
and maintaining balanced relaxation is the most vital and difficult physical
element involved in singing and speaking, it is given primary emphasis and
particular attention.

As detailed in the exercises that follow, the muscles of the larynx are generally divided into two groups: the *intrinsic muscles*, that is, those inside the
larynx, which directly control phonation, and the *extrinsic muscles*, that is,
those that move the larynx as a whole and keep it suspended in the neck. It
should be your aim to relax the latter set of muscles as well as all the outer
muscles above your shoulders, and then to maintain this relaxation while you
make sounds. By doing this, you are clearing the way to allow the inner muscles of the larynx to function without obstruction in the production of sound.
You need not worry about manipulating the inner muscles that control the
vocal folds, for the mere thought of speaking or singing is enough to alert
them into functioning—they operate unconsciously and not by direct manipulation. In a healthy throat, if the outer muscles are relaxed, the inner ones
will take care of themselves.

"This is all very well," you may say, "but how am I to know when these
outer muscles are really relaxed?" This is easier than it may seem, because it
is possible for us to feel most of these muscles with our fingers and to detect
tension in them. On the other hand, we have no external tactile contact
with the inner muscles. It is the muscles you can feel with your fingers that
must be relaxed.

Following is the step-by-step approach to relaxing the extrinsic muscle
groups surrounding the vocal mechanism, focusing on six specific areas. Not
every person will have the same tensions, and in some people they are difficult to detect. However, if the person does not—at the beginning of study—
become aware of where potential danger spots lie, bad habits and tension
may accumulate, which in later years can cause strained singing or speaking.
What may seem like a small lack of coordination now may, as we grow older,
develop into a severe handicap. By following this simple plan, a person can
readily detect and correct individual problems.

Preparing for the Relaxation Techniques

Sit in a comfortable position; try to cultivate an untroubled state of mind.
Do not hurry. Do not press. The very essence of the exercises that follow is
that they be done slowly, deliberately, without clock watching. An effective
way to prepare the mind and body before beginning is through progressive
relaxation. Close your eyes and allow your body to relax from the crown of
your head to the bottom of your feet, consciously releasing any tensions you

notice. You are then ready to begin a series of specific exercises to achieve relaxation of the areas that can inhibit healthy phonation.

Six Exercises in Relaxation

These exercises are to be used not just *before* you begin to speak or sing, but also *during* vocal exercises, on every vowel, and finally on all pitches throughout your range. If you can achieve this at the beginning of your study, you will have conquered a major part of your technical trouble at its source. These exercises are progressive, one through six; ideally, each earlier exercise should be maintained as you proceed through the sequence.

In performing the following exercises, remember to be gentle and deliberate, without forcing. Some areas of tension may release only through repetition over time.

1. The Muscles of the Face (see appendix A, figure 9)

With the pads of your fingers, slowly and gently massage the facial muscles starting at your hairline and forehead, and continuing downward to your cheeks, lips, and chin. Use circular motions with both hands and feel your skin and underlying muscle yielding to the gentle movement of your fingers. Spend time on areas that feel tight, such as your eyebrows and temples. As you massage your cheeks, let your jaw hang slack with your lips and teeth slightly apart. Feel as if the only thing stopping your jaw from falling further is the skin on your face. Allow the muscles to fall into as limp a condition as possible, as if you have no expression on your face at all.

Facial muscles that do not hold tension will allow and enhance the singer's ability to project a full range of expression and emotion.

Maintaining the relaxation of these facial muscles, proceed to the next area.

2. The Tongue (see appendix A, figure 10)

Let your tongue soften and allow it to come forward to rest slightly out of your mouth on your lower lip, as it might if you were unconscious. It is important for your tongue to gently fall forward by releasing muscular holding, rather than by pushing it forward with muscular effort. Now stretch your tongue further out of your mouth down toward your chin, stretching it at the back. You may feel a pull under your chin. Then let it release back to lie relaxed against or on the lower lip. Repeat this several times until you feel less pull.

The tongue muscle structure is most often at fault in interfering with the free emission of the voice. The tongue is a very large mass of muscles, covering the entire floor of the mouth and extending down to the hyoid bone, from which the larynx is suspended. The front part of the tongue, which we can actually see in our mouth, is a very small portion compared to the much larger part that extends down the throat. If it is tensed in any way (i.e., concave in the middle, retracted from the lower teeth or the sides of the mouth, or humped toward the roof of the mouth), the singer or speaker will be in trouble. Evidence of frontal-tongue tension indicates tension at the root of the tongue, thereby creating tension in all the surrounding musculature that we are trying to release.

Relaxation requires developing an awareness of that tension, then learning to let go. Freedom of the tongue will allow clear diction and easy articulation. The tongue must move for articulation, but it can move with ease.

Maintaining the relaxed facial and tongue muscles, move on to the next area.

3. The Swallowing (Suprahyoid) Muscles (see appendix A, figure 11)

The swallowing muscles (*digastric* and *mylohyoid* muscles) can be felt under the chin and are the main muscles responsible for elevating the larynx. They are strong muscles, and when they contract during phonation they can cause all kinds of vocal problems.

As a test, place both index fingers together in the center of the area under your chin. Swallow and you will feel downward pressure from the action of the swallowing muscles. Any hardening here during phonation is a sure sign of tension in these muscles and in the root of the tongue, and should be eliminated. It is vitally important that this area be kept relaxed, soft, and pliable during all phases of voice production. This can be checked so easily with the fingers that there is no excuse for tension here.

Keeping your tongue relaxed in your mouth, you can massage these swallowing muscles to help them soften and release. Place your thumbs or fingers of each hand in the center area under your chin. Gently press with an up-and-down motion, alternating each hand, pushing vertically into the swallowing muscles. Move your hands slightly on either side of center, until you have massaged the entire area under your jaw, using the jawbone as a boundary. The action is like kneading bread.

Freedom of the swallowing muscles allows the larynx to stay in its naturally low position and facilitates easy onset of sound.

Maintaining relaxation in the facial, tongue, and swallowing muscles, move on to the next area.

4. The Mandible (Jaw) (see appendix A, figure 12)

Find the "jaw hinge," which is in front of the ears. This is called the *Temporomandibular Joint or (TMJ)*. There must be ease of movement in this joint, and the jaw must be able to drop without resistance.

Now take your chin between your thumb and forefinger and move it up and down, at first slowly, and eventually faster. If you have completely relaxed the hinge muscles of your jaw, this exercise will give you no trouble. On first trying it, most persons find, however, that there is resistance in the jaw, particularly when moving it back to a closed position. Involuntarily, the jaw muscles are inclined to stiffen. Not until you are able to move your jaw freely up and down without the slightest resistance will you have accomplished the aim of this exercise. Maintain all of the relaxation you have established up to this point. Do not permit concentration on one relaxing exercise to cause you to neglect the others. Above all, take it easy.

The benefits of a released jaw are consistency of resonating space, easy articulation, and freedom in the vocal tract.

5. The Larynx (see appendix A, figures 11 and 13)

Find your larynx by gently placing your fingers flat against the front of your neck. Now swallow; your fingers should feel the larynx rise and fall. With the larynx in its naturally low position, place the thumb and forefinger of one hand on either side of the larynx, and lightly move it from side to side. Eventually it will move easily without clicking. This exercise should be approached gently at all times.

The muscles that attach to the larynx (and/or the hyoid bone above it) are known as strap muscles and are responsible for keeping the larynx suspended in the throat. These strap muscles should not bind, inhibit, or pull on the larynx, so that it can maintain its natural and relaxed position during phonation.

Freedom in the strap muscles allows the larynx to perform its full range of actions for speaking or singing.

Maintaining relaxation in the facial, tongue, swallowing, and jaw muscles, and the laryngeal area, move on to the next area.

6. The Neck and Head (see appendix A, figure 13)

Allow your head to fall forward with the chin toward your chest. There is no need to pull your head down; simply release it and let it fall with the pull of gravity. You should feel the weight of your head like a bowling ball. This weight will help stretch the back of your neck, allowing those muscles to slowly lengthen and your head to fall even further forward. Now bring your head back to its balanced position atop the spine as described in the section on posture in chapter 1.

Allow it to nod up and down lazily on the balance point while maintaining all the other relaxation areas.

Release of tension in the muscles of the neck enables a release in other muscular systems in the body, allowing the appropriate muscles to work in concert for phonation.

Practice these exercises while seated at first. Then take the standing posture you have learned and repeat them. Once you have become familiar with this routine, it is time to apply what you have learned to vocalizing.

Chapter 3

Phonation

*I*n this chapter, we are considering the complete action of phonation, that is, harmoniously functioning relaxation and breathing coupled with an added element that we call *support*. After you have mastered relaxation in the six areas mentioned and have learned to combine posture, diaphragm action, and rib cage stability in breathing, your next step is to use what you have learned to improve your speaking and singing voice. It is not enough merely to produce a pleasant sound. This sound must be controlled, supported, and sustained; in doing this correctly, you will call upon the action of a combination of the rib muscles, the pelvic and abdominal muscles, and the leg muscles running all the way down to the feet.

As you can see, the foregoing instructions are all directed toward control for the purpose of keeping the breath in steady and constant supply during speaking and singing. For some time, this will be a conscious act of co-coordinating, but with faithful practice it will gradually become second nature. Obviously such mastery cannot be developed overnight.

Do not attempt shortcuts. Do not expect to accomplish in a week what will require a year or more of close application. To produce a completely reliable singing and speaking technique, well-coordinated practice and muscular development will be needed. During this period of development, the attention and advice of an experienced teacher are indispensable.

Take the proper posture as described in chapter 1, making sure that all areas of relaxation have been checked. Draw in a breath with the mouth open. Allow the breath to go out the same way it was drawn in and with no change in the posture of the body or position of the mouth. Repeat several times. You will realize, of course, that the rib muscles at the back should still be stretched, never relaxing their firmness and, therefore, leaving the action of breathing to the diaphragm, abdominal wall, and lower supporting muscles.

Our first step toward correct phonation will consist of the emission of a very breathy, audible sigh. Almost all of us have a tendency to bring into play, consciously or unconsciously, some of the extrinsic throat muscles, which act to make the vocal folds approximate too closely (interfere with each other) when they are in vibration. The sigh we suggest will cause somewhat more breath than usual to pass between the folds while a light sound is being made. Now, with a vowel-sound in your mind (think "ah" for example) take in another breath. Emit it as an "ah," exactly as described above.

The student must not *force* air between the folds in this case, but *allow it to escape* in the most relaxed and lazy manner imaginable. After you have achieved true coordination of your vocal mechanism, you will no longer need to use this artificial method of assuring that the folds do not come together too closely. Your inner laryngeal muscles will have been coordinated and will have acquired the proper tonus to keep the folds vibrating optimally.

The breathy sigh described above is specifically used to coordinate the breath with the vocal folds. It is only the first step toward achieving a balanced onset of sound and is not to be confused with a breathy sound quality in the voice or use of a whisper.

After you get beyond the initial exercises given here and begin to say or sing syllables and then words, you should be certain that with each sound you make, you are focusing your eyes on a distant object. You should also use a mirror to sing or speak to, as an aid in projecting your voice and also to detect any strange habits involving facial grimaces or neck tensions. You must begin to consider your vocal efforts as a form of expression, exposition, or declaration. In other words, you do not make a study of phonation simply to speak or sing to yourself. You make sounds to *project your voice and your ideas*, be they dramatic, political, or musical, to other people.

Exercises for Phonation

1. With your posture maintained, tongue and muscles under your chin relaxed, take a few slow breaths. There should be no action of the rib cage or change in the limp position of the tongue during all the phonation exercises.

2. With all the previous instructions followed, take another breath and expel about half of it before making a sound. Now interrupt the expulsion of air with a very lazy and light sighing sound on "hah" beginning in the middle part of your voice and inflecting downward. Repeat this several times, checking carefully all six areas of relaxation, as well as your breathing and support.

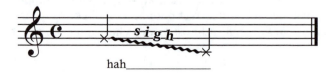

3. Repeat this exercise but with this difference: when you begin to sigh, allow your lips to open and close several times. The result will be a light hum. Do not think of this as an attempt to form the letter [m], however. Simply feel that you are interrupting the sigh, in which your mouth is slightly open, by drawing your lips together several times until your breath has been expelled. Make as loosely formed a conso- nant sound as possible. Do not bring your lips together firmly to form a tense [m]. The [m] used in this way helps you immeasurably to begin to think in terms of syllables, made up of both vowel and conso- nant sounds. The [m] is a voiced consonant, which means that while it is being pronounced, the vocal folds are vibrating. It is formed at the very front of the mouth without involving any other articulators such as the tongue or hard palate. It in no way has a tendency to disturb the desired relaxation when uttered as suggested:

hah-mah-mah-mah-mah

4. Repeat the previous exercise, but change the vowel sounds this time by making a pattern of the sounds "mah-meh-mee-moh-moo." Make every effort to maintain each vowel sound on its initial form as you would say it, without allowing it to become a diphthong:

ah (Father) eh (Get) ee (Meet) oh (Go) oo (Food)

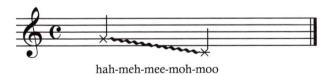

hah-meh-mee-moh-moo

5. Repeat, omitting the [m], but sustaining the sound. This will allow you to observe more carefully whether or not your tongue remains limp. A slight change in its position will be felt between vowels, but this should be minimal and not effected by you consciously. The posi- tion of the front of the tongue should not change.

6. Repeat, this time using a definite pitch in the lower-middle part of your voice. Start on about d, and *sing* the vowel sounds instead of say-

ing them. Continue this exercise by raising the pitch by half-steps, sustaining all the sounds on each pitch in turn, without progressing out of the middle part of the voice.

mah   meh   mee   moh   moo
ah   eh   ee   oh   oo

You are beginning to feel what it is to make relaxed vocal sounds. Your only concern should be with the *feeling in your throat* as you make these sounds. If the sounds are being produced completely without strain, you will have no feeling there at all.

We have merely touched on the basic exercises to be used while you are still very much concentrating on the areas of relaxation and the proper techniques of breathing discussed earlier. More exercises will be introduced in the following chapters.

Chapter 4

Freeing the Voice
from Song to Speech

Maria Argyros

Though we rely on our speaking voice continuously in everyday communication, few of us are conscious of how we use our voice. Likewise, most singers are much more aware of their singing technique than they are of their voice usage when speaking. We take our speaking voice for granted. However, speaking incorrectly can be more damaging to the larynx and vocal folds than singing incorrectly—simply because most of us speak more than we sing. Ideally, we should speak as we sing and sing as we speak, maintaining the same healthy techniques and principles for both.

Most problems in the speaking voice are caused by (1) speaking in a pitch range that is too low; (2) not breathing often enough and speaking without breath flow; and (3) speaking with too much tension and effort in the articulators of the mouth, including the tongue, lips, soft palate, and jaw. All of these problems can be greatly improved with the proper posture, spinal alignment, and rib suspension discussed in chapter 1. Breath management is a vital part of the formula for healthy voice use. Even when speaking, the vocal folds should vibrate with a steady flow of breath for the length of the phrase or sentence being spoken. Breath flow is accomplished more easily with the proper coordination and alignment of the body. Remember good posture when speaking!

The exercises in this chapter will guide you through a series of steps designed to help you understand and feel what you need to do to overcome these three major causes of problems with the speaking voice, and keep your voice healthy. Be prepared to experience some new feelings in your voice! For example, if you have been speaking in too low a pitch range, your voice will sound brighter or higher to you when you no longer produce the sound from

15

your throat. You will also experience more ease and flow when you speak. Your vocal identity will change, and as your voice changes, you will not recognize yourself. Be aware that changes in your *perception* of your voice are just as important as the physical changes—and both will require adjustments as you improve.

When you practice, allow yourself time to go through all the six areas of relaxation, paying close attention to the muscles around your mouth, tongue, and jaw. The goal is to avoid overuse and tensing in the articulators when speaking. Nothing should feel pushed or pressed. For this reason, you may have to slow down and ease up as you first begin to speak in a healthier way. Slowing down every word or phrase is suggested as a way to allow time to get to the source of the tension and process the new feelings. By putting your thumb under your chin while speaking, you will be able to feel the action of your swallowing muscles and root of your tongue. You will become aware of how much you may be overworking these muscles. If there is hardness under your chin or stiffness in your tongue, then you must learn to relax these muscles during phonation.

You are also encouraged to take frequent breaths to better enable the release of tension and assure that your speaking voice has a consistent supply of air to keep it from dropping in pitch. You know you are speaking too low when you hear a crackling sound in your voice, especially at the end of sentences. This is called "vocal fry" because it sounds similar to bacon frying in the pan. Vocal fry is a result of lack of breath flow while the vocal folds are vibrating and is very tiring and irritating to the voice.

Another sign of unhealthy vocal production is the frequency of glottal stops. This is when the vocal folds come together too forcefully, resulting in a slight catch or stop in the sound. They tend to occur in words that do not start with a consonant, such as "it," "in," or "at." Continual glottal stops are detrimental to the voice. Any tendency to speak in this manner will be eliminated with the new production you will practice in the following exercises. You will develop an ability to allow your voice to flow with breath, without excess effort in either your throat or your mouth.

A healthy speaking voice has the ability to use a range of about five pitches, which enables more resonance and clarity. Speaking on one low pitch (monotone) is fatiguing and boring, even unpleasant, to listen to. Finding one's optimum speaking-pitch range is very important, though it may vary at first until the voice is free enough to settle into its final comfortable range. If you tend to have excessive tension, you may start a little lower in the beginning of this process to assure relaxation and comfort. In time, your pitch range may come up a half- to whole-step. But do not rush. Start where there is the most relaxation and ease. In general, the speaking range of higher female voices is around middle-C to the G above. Higher male voices would be the same notes (C to G) in their own octave. Lower voices (alto or baritone) may find their range a whole-step or minor-third lower. Speaking with inflection and expression (using more than one pitch) gives the voice a melodic and pleasant quality. For this reason, we will find and develop your healthy speaking voice by way of your singing voice.

Finding Your Pitch

Let's begin. First, prepare yourself physically. After practicing the six areas of relaxation, add good posture by lengthening your spine and keeping your ribs suspended. Take several abdominal breaths, knowing that you will be using the breath as the power source for all phonation.

Next, begin warming up your voice by singing some gentle "*Hum-mum-mums*" on one low comfortable pitch (see chapter 3 on phonation). Be careful to start the sound on the *H* with a gentle release of your breath. The sound must be light—not pushed or forced. Allow the tongue to soften and lie in the bed of the mouth, with no tensing in the back. Try other vowels and vowel combinations while constantly checking for tension in the tongue. Breathe each time and keep the breath moving through the [m]. This should create a tickle or feeling of vibration in the nose or upper lip. If the *Hum* is sung correctly, you are already starting to make the changes necessary for healthy speech. You will soon start to feel your speaking voice where you feel the resonance of the *Hum—more forward and out of the throat.*

Keeping this sensation of easy and flowing phonation, now use the sentence "HOW ARE YOU TODAY?" in a variety of ways, as described below.

1. Sing the sentence on a moderately low pitch.

2. Sing it several times, each time paying attention to the following:

   a. make sure that your breath is flowing freely

   b. check for tension in your tongue while you pronounce the words, by putting your thumb under your chin to feel the action and movement of the swallowing muscles. You may feel the "flexing" of the muscles, but you should never have a hard or pressed feeling, which means you are working too hard to articulate the words.

3. If you are tensing your tongue during articulation, sing the sentence much slower and lighter, stretching out each syllable. Feel under your chin again to find and observe on which consonants your tongue is overworking. You must breathe often and stay on pitch:

   Hoowwwaaarrrreeeyyyyooooutoooodaayyy?

Repeat this several times, until your tongue can relax and become gentler in its movement. The words should glide from vowel to consonant on the breath flow; the consonant must not stop the flow. Once you have succeeded in feeling this connection from one word to the next, you can begin singing the sentence faster. Because there is more ease and flow, try to sing more words on the same breath, but never let yourself run out of breath completely before taking another. Always keep a constant supply of air, so it feels like the breath is carrying the sound. Also, keep checking for any added tension in all six areas of relaxation.

4. Sing the sentence on a descending five-note scale, in a comfortable lower, middle range.

How   are   you   to - day?

5. Repeat all of the instructions described above while singing the scale several times. If you feel too much tension, you may need to lower the scale by a half- or whole-step, and/or slow it down. Again, remember the breath flow and six areas of relaxation!

Now it is time to transition from singing to speaking.

6. In singsong speech (in the same pitch range and same feeling as in singing the five-note scale)—give each word a slight upward inflection. Do not stay on one pitch. Do not sing it.

HOW ARE YOU TO DAY

   a. Breathe when needed.

   b. Do not drop the pitch.

   c. Check for tensions in articulation.

7. In singsong speech, give each word the same upward inflection, but connect the words more on the breath flow, like a wavy line.

HOW ARE YOU TO DAY

   a. Vary the pitch from word to word.

   b. Check for tensions.

   c. Check your posture.

8. Repeat the sentence several times with a slight stress on a different word each time.

   HOW are you today   How ARE you today

   How are YOU today   How are you toDAY

   a. Breathe before each repetition.

   b. Keep the same wavy flow for inflection.

   c. If you drop the pitch, start again with more breath.

   d. Check for tongue stiffness on the stressed word or glottal stop on the word "are."

Now you are ready to try other sentences. Apply the same techniques to the short sentences listed below using this simple scale pattern:

Sentences with consonants that involve the lips in articulation:

1. Walt won't wait for Will, won't wait for Will.

2. Who or what is cool; oh, who is cool?

3. Magic moonbeams meet, the moonbeams meet.

4. Bernie builds a barn, he builds a barn.

5. Patty passed the pie, she passed the pie.

Sentences with consonants that involve the lips and teeth in articulation:

6. Father fed his flock, he fed his flock.

7. Knaves are very vain, they're very vain!

Sentences with consonants that involve the tongue and teeth in articulation:

8. Think a thought throughout, think it throughout.

9. They are with us there, they're with us there.

Sentences with consonants that involve the tip of the tongue and front of the hard palate in articulation:

10. Time and tide won't wait, the tide won't wait.

11. Dawn declares the day, declares the day.

12. Name an honest man, an honest man.

13. Leave the least to last, the least to last.

Sentences with consonants that involve the body of the tongue and the hard palate in articulation:

14. Roger rode his raft, he rode his raft.

15. Sing this silly song, this silly song.

16. Zany, zigzag lanes, zig-zig-zag lanes.

17. Shepherds shear their sheep, they shear their sheep.

18. Measure leisure well, measure it well.

19. You tell Yankee yarns, tell Yankee yarns.

Sentences with consonants that involve the body of the tongue and the soft palate in articulation:

20. Keep your cookies cool; oh, keep them cool.

21. Give the golden goose, the golden goose.

22. Jiggs lugs logs from bogs, lugs logs from bogs.

23. Singers sang a song, they sang a song.

24. Jingling bangles clang, the bangles clang.

25. Frank will thank the bank, he'll thank the bank.

Sentence with a consonant that involves the glottis and breath in articulation:

26. Henry honked his horn, he honked his horn.

Here are some suggestions for how to work with the above sentences. Take as much time as necessary to accomplish each step—knowing that those with more difficult vocal issues may need to spend more time on these beginning steps.

1. Sing each sentence on the scale passage indicated, taking a breath at the comma.

   a. This instills an awareness of the breath and builds the habit of breathing more frequently.

   b. This assures sufficient breath supply to enable relaxation of any tension in the articulators and throat.

2. Sing each sentence on the scale passage indicated and do not breathe at the comma.

   a. This requires adding more words on one breath, thus elongating the exhalation without adding tension.

   b. Do not let the consonants interrupt the flow.

3. In a singsong voice, keeping the same pitch range, speak each sentence with a breath at the comma.

   a. Elongate each word to be sure the tongue does not tense on the consonants and connect one word to the next with breath flow.

   b. Try to add wavy inflection.

   c. Be aware of the higher feeling of resonance.

   d. Take time to breathe abdominally each time.

4. In a singsong voice, keeping the same pitch range, speak each sentence and do not breathe at the comma.

   a. Use your breath to carry the sentence to the end with some inflection.

   b. Do not drop the pitch.

Additional Practice Techniques

By using your singing voice, hopefully you have experienced a new way to speak with more resonance, ease, and clarity. If you keep practicing, you will enjoy the benefits of this healthier production.

Making the transition from these formal exercises to your everyday speaking will take much awareness on your part. Use your new voice in conversation and in your daily life. You will notice that you must breathe more often in order to maintain your pitch range. It will take time to adjust to the higher feeling and sound of your healthier voice.

Here are some other ways to practice using your new speaking voice:

- Count numbers in groups of 3 or 5 numbers at a time in your singsong voice. Add more numbers on a single breath without dropping the pitch or adding tension. Use lots of energy and practice good posture. You may also sing the numbers on a single low pitch to help, applying all the techniques you have practiced in the sentences.

- Read paragraphs from a newspaper or magazine. Breathe frequently, especially at the punctuation marks. Can you keep your new voice consistently? Are there glottal stops? Do you have inflection? Project and energize the words as though you were speaking in a large room or hall.

- Think of a story and tell it to a friend (real or imaginary). Try to use your new voice as you tell the story. Let your voice ride along on the breath and use inflection.

Reminders for Good Voice Use

Below are some basic technical points to remember as you go through the process of changing your speaking voice. Pick one point at a time to focus on, and practice in your daily life until you have incorporated and conquered all of them. Always go back to these basics if you are having trouble maintaining your speaking voice in your pitch range:

- Speak on the breath flow.
- Take frequent abdominal breaths.
- Maintain good posture (spinal alignment and suspended ribs).
- Maintain optimum pitch level (Hum).
- Avoid vocal fry.
- Avoid glottal stops.
- Keep a lazy tongue and soft swallowing muscles in articulation.

Spend some time working with the exercises in this chapter to gain comfort with these concepts. The next chapter will describe articulation and introduce more complex sentences for your practice.

Chapter 5

Articulation of Consonants in Detail

 𝓔dmund J. Myer, a famous teacher writing late in the nineteenth century, said, "Consonants are the bones of speech." He could not have said it more aptly, for without consonants there *is* no speech. Those who think they can slur over their consonants in singing or speaking are failing to utilize one of the most important assists in vocal communication and expression.

How often we are prompted to ask a friend, "What did you say?" when he or she seems to be speaking in a loud-enough voice? And how many times have we attended recitals, lectures, or plays during which we had to strain our ears to understand the performer? Neglect of consonant articulation is not the only fault that may handicap a speaker or singer and annoy his or her audience—but it is, by all odds, the most prevalent omission. If the "bones" of phonation are neglected, the listener can spend the whole evening guessing how to fill in the gaps between the vowel sounds.

The human voice is the only musical "instrument" that can combine the meaning of speech with the meaning of music by means of words. In forming words, the articulators (tongue, hard and soft palates, lips and teeth) combine vowel with consonant sounds.

We can tell whether an animal is frightened or happy—or perhaps sounding a warning—by the tone of its voice. It can register its emotion, but communication stops there; it cannot tell us the source of its joy, fear, or pain, or what it wants us to do about it. It takes both tone and words to convey meaning. People communicate with words, along with nuances in dynamics and tone quality, to form a truly differentiated interpretation of meanings and moods. This point seems to have escaped many singers and speakers who are capable of showing change of emotion in sound, but are unable to communicate adequately because of careless enunciation.

Having practiced the complete relaxation described in chapter 2, readers may well feel that if and when they enunciate clearly, they may endanger the nice framework for phonation that they have achieved and may trip over all sorts of tensions that can develop to interfere with even the best voice production. That is the reason for this chapter on articulation—the use of the articulators and musculature above the larynx in interrupting the flow of vibrating breath to form the various sounds we recognize as consonants. (Strictly speaking, we should acknowledge that vowels, too, are articulated, but only because the articulating organs act naturally to change the size and shape of the mouth cavity and pharynx to differentiate the vowel sounds.)

The articulators assume different adjustments in relation to each other so that they act as valves whose opening and shutting form consonants. These adjustments can be classified in many complicated ways, but we can simplify them by observing that they are characterized particularly in three ways: (1) position, (2) whether or not they are accompanied by vibration of the vocal folds, and (3) duration. Each of these factors is discussed below.

Position

In discussing the positions of the articulators it is helpful to simplify matters by dividing the consonants into those produced by the action of the lips, and are called *labials*, and those produced by the action of the tongue, and are called *linguals*.

The labials in turn may be divided into two groups:

1. Those in which the lips alone are used, as in the following examples:

[w]	w	win
[hw]	wh	which
[m]	m	meet
[p]	p	pork
[b]	b	bee

2. Those in which the lips are used in conjunction with the teeth:

[f]	f	father
[v]	v	very

The linguals may be divided into four groups:

1. Those formed by tongue and teeth:

[θ]	th	thick
[ð]	th	that

2. Those formed by the tip of the tongue and the hard palate:

[t]	t	tip
[d]	d	do
[n]	n	no

[l]	l	lip
[r]	r	ripe (flipped)

3. Those formed by the body of the tongue and the hard palate:

[s]	s	sow
[z]	z	zebra
[ʃ]	sh	show
[ʒ]	zh	azure
[j]	y	yes
[ɹ]	r	row (American)

4. Those formed by the body of the tongue and the soft palate:

[k]	c	cat
[k]	k	king
[g]	g	get
[ŋ]	ng	sing

"American" R [ɹ] is produced by the central part of the tongue moving toward the hard palate.

Vibration of the Vocal Folds

This brings us to the second factor involved in the characterization of consonants: that is, whether they are voiced or unvoiced. A *voiced consonant* is one whose pronunciation is accompanied by the vibration of the vocal folds:

[b]	b	bead		[w]	w	west
[d]	d	deed		[m]	m	me
[g]	g	good		[n]	n	not
[v]	v	virtue		[l]	l	lot
[ð]	th	this		[r]	r	red
[z]	z	zoo		[j]	y	year
[ʒ]	zh	azure		[ŋ]	ng	sing

An *unvoiced consonant* is one which is emitted without any accompanying vibration of the vocal folds:

[p]	p	pea
[t]	t	tea
[k]	c	cow
[k]	k	key
[f]	f	fall
[θ]	th	thought
[s]	s	see
[ʃ]	sh	she
[hw]	wh	which
[h]	h	hot

Duration

The third factor in determining the quality of a consonant is the length of time involved in its emission. Consonants either stop abruptly, in which case they are called *stops*, or they continue and are therefore called *continuants*.

Stops:

[p]	p	ape	[d]	d	date
[b]	b	bottle	[k]	k	kite
[t]	t	at	[g]	g	gate

Continuants:

[w]	w	we	[j]	y	you
[hw]	wh	where	[r]	r	rose
[m]	m	music	[s]	s	seal
[f]	f	fate	[ʃ]	sh	shower
[v]	v	vale	[z]	z	zealous
[ð]	th	those	[ʒ]	zh	azure
[n]	n	nice	[θ]	th	thistle
[l]	l	leap	[ŋ]	ng	song
			[h]	h	horse

Needless to say, this is a very simplified classification of consonants, but it should suffice to understand what is involved in their formation. You will notice that we are concerned not with spelling but with sound, since *cat* and *kite* are initially the same phonetically—just as *leisure*, *azure* and *mirage* all contain the same sound [ʒ].

Exercises

For the pronunciation of consonants as exercises, begin by establishing the same conditions of relaxation and coordination that have been set forth up to this point. After you have satisfied yourself that you are ready for correct phonation, practice at first only the few words, which have been used as examples in the foregoing. You will see that, no matter how much you move your lips (as, for example, in *which* or *west*) it will be unnecessary to disturb the relaxation of the extrinsic muscles of the throat.

Next, try saying or singing, *mah-nah-ng-ah* slowly. These sounds start at the front of the mouth using only the lips and proceed from there to the use of the tongue, first employing its tip in conjunction with the hard palate, then its body in connection with the soft palate. You will notice that no matter how fast you say or sing these sounds, it is possible (as it is indeed imperative) to maintain freedom.

Working with More Complex Sentences

Once you have a good foundation, it is time to apply these techniques to longer and more difficult sentences. When working with the sentences that follow, take a breath every two or three words at first, if necessary, until you eliminate tensions in your articulation of the consonants. You may discover that you are pressing your lips together too tightly for certain consonants. Explore how the tongue must move for every specific consonant indicated in each sentence. The tongue interacts with the hard palate, teeth, or soft palate, depending on the consonant. Work on those consonants where the tongue feels the least flexible.

Learn to move all the articulators with less effort. When articulation feels easier, start to connect more words together. Avoid glottal stops and vocal fry, as these are signs of lack of breath flow. Always take a new breath and start again. Be aware of the possibilities for inflection and variation in pitch as you speak these sentences. You may also begin by singing the sentences on one pitch and then moving into singsong speaking as suggested in chapter 4.

Following the order given in the simple outline of consonant characteristics, below is a series of sentences designed to make specific use of one set of articulators.

To begin with the articulation of the lips, try saying the following sentence clearly and distinctly and slowly at first, being sure to maintain throat relaxation while speaking the words without exaggerating the movements of the mouth:

[w] (w) A coward weeps and wails with woe when his wiles are thwarted.

Now try this one, observing the difference in effect due to lack of vocal fold vibration, although the same articulators are working:

[hw] (wh) Which whelp whined when he heard the whale wheeze?

Notice that in both of the cases above the consonant sound is a continuant. Now, still employing the lips specifically, say the following sentence, observing that the consonant sound is both voiced *and* a continuant:

[m] (m) Men and women may swim in the warm summertime before September storms come upon them.

The following two sentences again contain words requiring lip action, but both consonants are stops. The *b*, however, is voiced, while the *p* is not:

[b] (b) The big, bold baboon grabbed the bare branches with his bony, brown hands.

[p] (p) The pelican's pouch is primarily appropriate for keeping him supplied with supper.

The following sentences still involve the use of the lips, but here in conjunction with the teeth. Notice the difference in effect between the unvoiced *f* sounds and the voiced *v*'s:

[f] (f) Five elephants huffed and puffed as they filed through the Friday traffic followed by a laughing waif.

[v] (v) Vivacious voices strove to give more volume to the various verses.

The next sentences call attention to the linguals of the first group; that is, those formed by the interaction of tongue and teeth. The first sentence uses unvoiced sounds; the next one, voiced sounds:

[θ] (th) A thousand thoughts about birth and death came thronging to the mind of the thin, unhealthy youth.

[ð] (th) They scythed the withering grass beside the smooth paths.

Our next examples point up the use of the tip of the tongue and the hard palate. As you read these phrases aloud, try to think carefully about the use of the articulators mentioned. Also be sure to maintain as much relaxation as possible through the entire throat area, so that the articulators may remain flexible and you will feel in no way "tongue-tied" when you have finished.

[t] (t) Try to take the time to teach Patty a pleasant tune.

[tʃ] (ch) Cheerful Cheshire cats chew chunks of chopped chicken and choke down chestnuts and cheese.

You will feel when speaking this sentence that your tongue is still using its tip for pronunciation of the *ch*, but it also uses its body in relation to the hard palate. This, then, is a combination of the sounds of *t* [t] and *sh* [ʃ].

[d] (d) Day after day, the good old educators tried to din adequate knowledge into dreamy dunces.

[n] (n) An honest scientist needs no hindrance in his sound investigation into the wonders of the universe.

[l] (l) Violins and lutes played lovely tunes as the pale silver moonlight filtered through the olive trees.

[r] (r) Ripe, round, bright, red berries drenched with rich cream provide thorough pleasure to those who truly relish fruit.

Try saying this last sentence aloud; first using a flipped r [r], which involves the tip of the tongue in contact with the hard palate. Then notice the difference when you read it using the standard American r [ɹ], which actually involves raising the body of the tongue toward the roof of the mouth. Avoid using the lips to pronounce r [ɹ]; this is not necessary. Depending on whether you are a singer or a public speaker, a radio announcer or an actor— or if you wish simply to give particular emphasis to a word here or there— you may find yourself using the flipped r [r]. Singers especially find that it can help enormously to clarify a word if used initially and that it provides a quick springboard to a following vowel when used in the body of a word. You will notice that French singers use it when singing their own songs, although they speak with an [R], which is pronounced far back in the throat, almost gargled, in fact. Americans should learn to use the flipped r [r], but be careful to use it judiciously and not in such a way as to sound exaggerated or affected.

The next sentences illustrate the interaction of the body of the tongue and the hard palate:

1. [s] (s) Susan sighed softly as she passed the nice Swiss physicist in the passageway.

2. [z] (z) At the zoo the lazy visitors observed zebras, gazelles, lizards, and prize lions.

3. [ʃ] (sh) She shed her mesh shoes and shamelessly shook her freshly washed shawl from her shoulders.

4. [ʒ] (zh) We usually derive composure and pleasure from leisure.

5. [dʒ] (j or g) The jealous major became enraged at the adjutant's jolly jokes about his huge budget.

6. [j] (y) Last year the yew in the canyon beyond your yard turned yellow.

7. [ɹ] (r) Ripe, round, bright, red berries drenched with rich cream provide thorough pleasure to those who truly relish fruit.

Coming to the use of the body of the tongue in conjunction with the soft palate, try the following:

1. [k] (c and k) The kindly king and his quiet queen liked pickled pig's knuckles with their cooked cabbage and crusty kidney pie.

2. [g] (g) The ghastly ghost ogled the gaping guests, then wagged its gray finger at them as it gathered the garnets together.

3. [ŋ] (ng) Bring me a spring song to sing for the waiting throng.

Now notice the difference in pronunciation of the ng sound in the next sentence, where it is necessary to follow it with an additional sound of g:

4. [ŋg] (ng) The distinguished Englishman learned the Anglo Saxon language and wrote singular jingles in it.

In the sentence below, we hear the ng sound again, but this time with a following k:

5. [ŋk] (ngk) The monkey blinked and wrinkled his pink nose as he tinkled the clinking trinkets on his ankles.

H [h] is rather special, as it is produced simply by breath passing between the vocal folds.

1. [h] (h) Harry the hunter hasn't hiked home through the hills since he heard that a huge horse's hoof print was beheld in Hiram's Hollow.

Once you have eliminated all tensions from these sounds, try speaking the sentences aloud as if you were addressing an audience. The greater dynamics will be accomplished not by greater effort in the articulators or throat but with greater breath energy and body involvement.

Now it is time to utilize this technique in any other spoken material that you may have occasion to use. This could include monologues, scripts, poetry, business presentations, sermons, lectures, and speeches. If you are studying a poem or a speech, do not rush in and attempt to convey its innermost meanings or emotions at the first reading. Say it phrase by phrase, thinking about your posture, relaxation, breathing, enunciation, and projection, and testing these factors one by one. As you progress, you may find yourself taking fewer breaths, emphasizing words differently, or using more inflection.

Chapter 6

Vocalizing with the McClosky Technique

Maria Argyros

ny student of singing should know and understand how the human voice functions. Such knowledge can help inspire a sense of respect and wonder at how many intricate muscles work together to give us our method of communication, expression, and connection to each other through language and sound.

The natural voice is a perfect creation. All a singer has to do is remove his or her bad habits, tensions, and other conditions that obstruct the true potential of sound that is already there. Attaining this freedom is a gradual process. All of the exercises in this book thus far are designed to get you started on releasing tensions in the muscles of the vocal apparatus and allowing the vocal folds to coordinate with and respond to the breath flow in an unencumbered and natural manner. These first exercises, in the chapters on relaxation and song-to-speech techniques, are a superb guide to learning how to accomplish this freedom and coordination. Such careful attention to the proper function and vibration of the vocal folds is vital and constitutes the very foundation that can assure maintenance of a healthy voice for a lifetime. For these reasons, the first step in a singer's voice training or healing is to accomplish the exercises on phonation, breathing, and relaxation described thus far in this book. Having established this solid foundation, one can begin developing the full potential of his or her voice.

The next step in the developmental process is to expand to other vocal exercises that require longer phonation while still maintaining the basics. At this early stage, singing short patterns without consonants, and staying in the middle range, enables the singer to maintain the foundational aspects of the technique without challenging the voice to go farther than it can without strain or tension. Because the singer is still learning the basics of the tech-

31

nique, "vocalizing with the technique" means that each exercise being sung should be repeated several times while monitoring the body's posture and breathing, and also checking for tensions in all six areas of relaxation.

What is important is the quality of the sound. The McClosky Technique requires the singer to develop an awareness of his or her entire body, especially the condition of the muscles that influence the voice most directly. Discerning quality and ease of movement is extremely important, because quality of movement determines quality of sound. One can monitor the body by using one's own hands as a tactile tool to help recognize tension and maintain coordination. With keen awareness, the singer can feel the difference when tension is released and tell when the body is functioning more efficiently. For these reasons, and as advised by Mr. McClosky himself, it is helpful to "Keep Your Hands Busy" while singing—advice better known to students of the McClosky Technique as "KYHB"! In this way we are focusing on the process, not the product, thereby clarifying cause and effect.

There are several ways to develop awareness during phonation. For example (as explained in chapter 1), in order to ensure that the ribs do not collapse and that the breath is moving, the singer can put one hand on his or her sternum and the other on the abdomen at the naval or natural waistline. It then becomes very easy to feel whether the chest and ribs are stable, and whether the abdominal muscles are moving inward on the exhalation. Another way to ensure that the rib cage does not collapse is to put one's hands on the lower ribs on both sides and keep them there while singing. The presence of the hands will help make the singer aware of the ribs and their position.

To help relax the jaw hinge and chewing muscles, it is helpful to touch the face lightly on either side at the cheekbones and down to the lower teeth area. The fingers should be slightly bent and never rigid. This is a gentle reminder to the jaw and facial muscles to stay relaxed while singing. It can also be helpful to gently massage the facial muscles while singing to keep the jaw released and tension from reoccurring. Once this is achieved, the singer should be able to move the jaw easily up and down with his or her hands while singing, as described in the fourth area of relaxation.

The swallowing muscles, which can be felt under the chin, are a real problem area for tension. This area also involves the root of the tongue. Fortunately these muscles can be easily monitored with a light touch under the chin to check for hardness or stiffness. Feeling hardness here gives the singer very tangible information that the back of the tongue is tensing. It is also possible to gently massage these muscles to help them stay soft while singing lightly (area 3). Of course, the body of the tongue must stay soft and forward in the mouth at all times. The tongue stretch will help the singer accomplish this (area 2).

The neck muscles often pull or tense while singing. The singer can put his or her hands lightly on either side of the larynx to help the strap muscles in the front of the neck relax, and then try gently moving the larynx while singing (area 5). Putting one's hands on the back of the neck behind the ears and near the base of the skull will help prevent those strong neck muscles from pulling. Release of tension here will better enable the head to stay balanced on the spine and prevent the chin from jutting forward (area 6). If there is tension in the mouth or lips, putting a finger on the upper lip or corners of the mouth will help to eliminate excessive movement in this area. The facial massage can also help with this (area 1).

Indeed, this hands-on approach provides the singer with valuable tools for dealing with tension as well as a way to address habits specifically and tangibly so that real change can take place. Once the correct body position is learned, or the relaxation is recognized, the use of hands can be gradually eliminated.

Using a mirror is very helpful for obtaining visual information on what the body is doing. A full-length mirror is useful for checking posture and body alignment, while a smaller mirror can be used to observe tension in the face, neck, and tongue.

Vocalizing Exercises

Now it is time to vocalize, remembering to continually monitor the body as part of the process. The four basic vocal patterns to begin with are:

1. Five-note scale descending

2. Three-note scale

3. Five-note scale

4. Triad

These patterns can be used in myriad ways, depending on what areas the singer needs to improve and how severe existing vocal problems may be. They may be used over and over to achieve freedom, ease, and maximum resonance in the voice. Start each pattern in a lower, comfortable range, and move up by a half-step with each repetition.

One of the most important goals of vocal training is learning to sing the five prominent Italian vowel sounds

ah	father
eh	bed
ee	meet
oh	obey
oo	soon

without manipulation or excessive change in the mouth or tongue. This has already been addressed in chapters 3, 4, and 5 of this book, but now it is time to begin exploring each vowel separately and releasing any tension in the tongue, face, or jaw with each vowel. Some vowels will feel easier than others at first. All of the following exercises can be used in any order and must be revisited and practiced again and again as production changes and tensions improve.

Note: Always start the sound with a release of breath to assure a balanced, easy onset of tone.

Example: Sing one vowel at a time on each of the scale patterns noted above. Sing one pattern at a time and do not rush. Repeat and move up by a half-step, staying in a comfortable middle range. Breathe each time and maintain breath flow. Check the six areas of relaxation on each of the five vowels.

hah _____
heh _____
hee _____
hoh _____
hoo _____

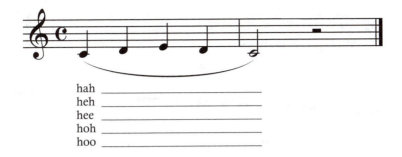

hah _____
heh _____
hee _____
hoh _____
hoo _____

hah _____
heh _____
hee _____
hoh _____
hoo _____

hah   eh   ee   oh   oo

Find the Best Vowel

By placing the thumb in the fleshy area under the chin, you can determine which vowel causes the least tension. The goal is to find the sound with the least muscle involvement in starting or keeping the sound. The tone will find the most natural resonance because it is most free. This vowel, once found, can be used as a guideline with which to align all the other vowels.

Example: Alternate the best vowel with each of the other vowels while singing any of the suggested scale patterns. For instance, if "ah" is the freer vowel, then sing the "ah" first, followed by another vowel. Each vowel should flow from one to the other smoothly without excessive changes in the tongue or mouth. Maintain breath flow and stay in the middle range.

hah	eh	ah	eh	ah
hah	ee	ah	ee	ah
hah	oh	ah	oh	ah
hah	oo	ah	oo	ah

When this sequence can be sung with ease, extend the pattern to a five-note scale.

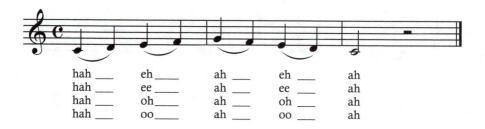

hah ___	eh___	ah ___	eh ___	ah
hah ___	ee ___	ah ___	ee ___	ah
hah ___	oh___	ah ___	oh ___	ah
hah ___	oo___	ah ___	oo ___	ah

hah	eh	ah	eh	ah	eh	ah	eh	ah
hah	ee	ah	ee	ah	ee	ah	ee	ah
hah	oh	ah	oh	ah	oh	ah	oh	ah
hah	oo	ah	oo	ah	oo	ah	oo	ah

Monitor for tensions in the mouth and tongue, or hardness in the swallowing muscles. Maintain breath flow and "KYHB" while singing. You may move up by half-steps as long as you can maintain the relaxation and breath flow.

Change the order and combination of the vowels while singing any of the patterns. The same feeling of flow with no manipulation should occur with each variation. All six areas of relaxation must be constantly checked until each vowel is free. The face and mouth must look and feel relaxed for each vowel.

Freeing and aligning the vowels will take time and patience. When this is achieved, it is time to challenge the body by expanding the patterns, while maintaining freedom in the six areas, and keeping the posture and breath-flow consistent.

Example: Sing two (or three) three-note scales on one breath, or two (or three) five-note scales on one breath with a different vowel on each scale. Try various combinations, and alternate vowels.

hee	oh
hah	oh
heh	ah

The Skip Pattern

Example: Sing a triad pattern on one vowel. Try all five vowels.

hah
heh
hee
hoh
hoo
hah   eh   ah   eh   ah

(If a shorter skip is necessary to maintain freedom, use a major third pattern first 1-3-1-3-1.)

hah
heh
hee
hoh
hoo
hah   eh   ah   eh   ah

Now alternate from one vowel to another, as explained above for the scale patterns. Monitor and check for tongue, mouth, and jaw tension. Breath flow and posture may be more difficult to maintain because of the skips. Keep the breath flowing into the second and third notes of the pattern, and KYHB!

Pairing Consonants with Vowels

All of the exercises so far are very basic and are suggested primarily to assure that the "foundation" of the voice is built and that good habits and correct perceptions are developed. For these reasons, we have dealt only with vowels to achieve the freest emission of tone without interruption.

When we sing without words we can appreciate the beauty of the sound, similar to any instrument. But the ability to convey ideas through words is unique to the art of singing. Words require consonants, which are formed by various combinations and interactions of the articulators, including the tongue, lips, teeth, soft palate, and hard palate. Freedom in these articulators becomes very important, because they must interact with each other efficiently, quickly, and with ease. Consonants need not interrupt the continuity of the tone. The tongue is the most prominent and active of the articulators and can also be the most problematic. The singer must become aware of how the tongue moves in the mouth and what other articulators are involved for each consonant or combination of consonants (see chapter 5).

Now it is time to go back to the first exercises, which were sung with all the vowels. Follow the instructions as before, but now pair a consonant with each vowel and try to achieve the same feeling of connection and flow with the consonant included in the pattern. Extend the pattern if you can.

Take time and do not rush the process. Explore all of the consonants and work with all the articulators involved to achieve ease of movement for each. Combine or alternate different consonants with different vowels. A consonant can be sung on every note of the pattern, or on every other note. If there is still tension, try just one consonant at the start of the pattern. Then add more.

The most important thing is to keep checking the swallowing muscles by putting your thumb under your chin to feel for hardness. Allow your tongue to move easily. Also, keep the lips and jaw relaxed while the tongue is moving independently inside the mouth. Always be aware of posture and breathing.

Example: On a three-note scale, sing various vowels with different consonants such as:

```
weh ____    weh ____    weh
lee ____    lee ____    lee
fah ____    fah ____    fah
goh ____    goh ____    goh
```

On a five-note scale sing:

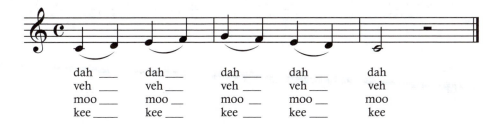

dah ___	dah ___	dah ___	dah ___	dah
veh ___	veh ___	veh ___	veh ___	veh
moo ___	moo ___	moo ___	moo ___	moo
kee ___	kee ___	kee ___	kee ___	kee

Then a triad in similar fashion:

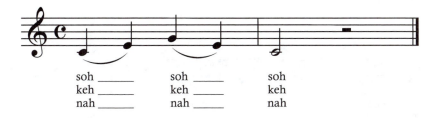

soh _____	soh _____	soh
keh _____	keh _____	keh
nah _____	nah _____	nah

Advanced Vocalization

The final goal of vocal development is acquiring the ability to sing freely and maintain the principles of the techniques while expanding the range of the voice, sustaining notes, improving resonance, and building stamina. If the singer succeeds in maintaining freedom in the extrinsic muscles while keeping good posture for breath management, then the voice will function freely, with nothing to inhibit or interfere with its natural ability to grow and flourish. Be assured that from this foundation, the full potential of the voice will emerge.

At this more advanced stage, bodily energy and strength become very important in helping to maintain and enhance the power and agility of the sound. The respiratory and posture muscles must be strong and well coordinated. More difficult vocalizations should now be practiced—such as the nine-note scale on all vowels, the arpeggio (repeated), and octave skips. Sustaining high notes on the breath, and singing patterns several times on one breath, are good ways to build stamina.

Vocalizing for increased range and flexibility—move up or down by half-step:

mee_____   meh ____   mah____   moh ____   moo ____

mee _____   meh _____   mah _____   moh _____   moo _____

Finally, the Song!

It is important to choose songs thoughtfully and carefully, so that the pieces chosen will help you advance comfortably and not require going beyond your current technical ability and range to accomplish the demands of the piece.

As with the exercises, one's repertoire should gradually increase in difficulty. Beginning pieces should have a simple melody in the middle range with an even, legato line. Then songs with increased melodic demands—such as bigger skips and added notes to extend range—can be introduced. More demanding pieces would require longer phrases, higher tones, larger and more frequent skip patterns, increased articulation demands, and moving patterns. Finally, material suited for the advanced singer would include coloratura passages, use of a wider range, requiring maintenance of tessitura and sustaining notes in the extremes of the range, sustained phrases, more complex rhythms, and language with difficult articulation demands.

How to Work on a Song

Preparing a song takes time and careful practice. There are several factors that comprise a song such as the text (words), melody, rhythm, tempo, dynamics, phrasing, articulation, accompaniment, and of course, the vocal sound. The singer must spend time to learn each of these components, one at a time, until it can all eventually come together into a complete expression of art.

The focus and purpose of this book is to give the singer tangible ways to improve his or her vocal production. The following practice steps are meant to continue this focus on vocal technique. Of course, the musical, language, and dramatic skills required of a singer must be part of the overall training but will not be addressed here. Other artistic issues are discussed in chapter 8 of this book.

It is important to understand that the same careful process for vocalizing we have explained and described in this chapter can and must also be applied to the process of learning to sing a song well. Remember to check all six areas of relaxation while singing a scale. Remember how important it is to use your hands to keep checking these areas for tension while singing (KYHB). Remember to articulate the consonants easily and quickly. Remember to maintain good posture and breath flow. When working on a song, these same foundational steps must be incorporated and practiced in the same way.

- *Listen to the song and study the music.*

   Begin by listening to the entire song to get an idea of the flow of the melody and rhythm. Look at the music and analyze where the vocal challenges may lie.

- *Sing the melody slowly on one vowel.*

   The first step to learning the song is to sing the melody notes on a single vowel. After working on some of the exercises at the beginning of this chapter, the singer should have accomplished some degree of freedom while singing all the vowels. Choose the vowel that has the least tension and most ease. The melody can be sung slowly and easily (not in strict rhythm) while checking each of the six areas of relaxation. Divide the piece into short, manageable phrases. In a more difficult song, it might be necessary to break it down into even smaller units, perhaps measure by measure. This is the time to check your posture and rib cage stability while singing. Be sure to monitor your swallowing muscles while moving from note to note to be sure there is no hardening there. Large intervals in the melody can be a place where your neck can tense or your jaw stiffen. Release your jaw (area 4) while singing. Use of your hands softly touching your face at the jaw hinge will help. Do gentle nods with your head to keep your neck free (area 6). Breath flow must not stop no matter what the melody pattern. Frequent breaths might be necessary at this beginning stage to maintain freedom.

- *Sing the melody in rhythm with phrasing.*

Once a good sense of flow in the melody notes is acquired, it is time to sing the song on one vowel in the exact rhythm that has been written. The singer must coordinate the intake of air to keep in time with the music. This may require taking a breath quickly at times. There should be no abdominal tightening while taking a breath in rhythm, or collapse of the rib cage while sustaining notes. Check again for tensions or changes in the six areas of relaxation. Several repetitions are in order to get free in each area and stay physically coordinated.

- *Sing melody on vowels of the words without consonants.*

Now it is time to incorporate the text. First, look at the words of the song and determine the primary vowel in every syllable. This will be tricky, depending on the language. For instance, English and German have several diphthongs (two vowel sounds within one syllable). It is important to elongate the prominent vowel in the syllable as the language dictates. The Italian language often has more than one vowel per syllable. For all languages, a sense of flow from one vowel to another with little effort or manipulation is the goal while singing words. Now it is time to sing the melody of the song (broken down into phrases) with only the vowels of each word (or syllable) without the consonants. Add breaths where it works well with the words (often at a punctuation mark such as a comma or period). Certainly it is easy to take a breath where there is a rest written in the music.

The vowels in the words require the singer to sing different vowel combinations. Each vowel may present its own potential for tension. Check the muscles of the face (area 1). Try to go from vowel to vowel with a relaxed mouth, even when moving the lips for "oh," for instance, or on the "ee" vowel where singers tend to tighten the mouth or tongue. Now repeat the phrase while checking the muscles under your chin (area 3). If a particular vowel tends to tense here, practice this vowel separately to get more freedom in your tongue and swallowing muscles. Then go back to the word in the song.

Remember, your jaw must not be set or rigid for any vowel. Try gently moving your larynx (area 5) while singing to also help free your voice on changing vowels. If a particular vowel is troublesome, always check posture and breathing. In general, vowels tend to tense when the air flow is lacking. Maintaining breath flow on each note of the phrase always helps in the relaxation process.

- *Add the consonants.*

Of course, words are not complete without the *consonants*! This brings another technical component into the process—articulation. The articulation of consonants must not interfere with the flow of the vocal sound achieved so far with the vowels. Become aware of how the articulators interact with each other as described in the chapter on articulation. Above all, the tongue must move without stiffness. Tensions may occur in any word or phrase during this final stage of learning a song. Certain vowels combined with certain consonants can pose problems depending on the singer. It is important to go back to the basics of checking the six areas of relaxation, and breath and posture.

Another factor when adding the consonants is the *onset* of the tone. This is where many singers overarticulate or forget to release the breath with the consonant to start the first word of the phrase. These physical signs of tension affect the quality of the sound and ease of production. Again, relaxation and coordination must define the process.

- *Sing words with consonants on one note.*

  An excellent way to help achieve a flow from word to word is to sing the words of the song on one note (in a comfortable middle range). Sing from consonant to adjoining vowel smoothly and easily as the breath flows out. Go slowly and breathe frequently. It is easy to feel the connection of the words and to detect any consonants that may be interrupting the line. Be sure to "lighten up" on those consonants and keep relaxation in the vowels.

- *Sing words on one note in exact rhythm.*

  Next, sing the words on one note again, but in exact rhythm, including all the breaths and rests. Try to keep the same sense of flow from syllable to syllable. Be aware of adding unnecessary movement in the ribs, shoulders, neck, or mouth when taking a breath.

- *Sing the melody, rhythm, and words together.*

  The final step is to go back to the song and try to sing the written melody and words with the same ease and flow that singing on one note provided. Be especially careful on skip patterns and florid patterns. As always, check for tensions in the six areas of relaxation, posture, rib cage maintenance, and breath flow.

Applying the basic principles of the McClosky Technique requires careful attention but will never fail. Freedom in the voice will enable freedom of expression through song and will be the singer's reward and greatest pleasure.

Summary of Steps to Learning a Song Vocally

1. Listen to the song and study the music for patterns and structure.
2. Sing the melody of the song slowly on one vowel to learn the notes and establish flow.
3. Sing the melody of the song on one vowel in the written rhythm. Add breath marks for phrasing.

4. Sing the melody of the song on only the vowels of each word without consonants.

5. Sing the words with the consonants on one note (in the middle range) for flow.

6. Sing the words with consonants on one note in exact rhythm with established breaths.

7. Sing the melody, rhythm, and words as written.

Chapter 7

Resonance and Color

$\mathcal{S}$tudents should have an adequate knowledge of their own instrument—including how it works and how to work it—before asking them to use it as a means of expression. No Olympic skater would be asked to go out on the ice and perform a complicated routine without a long period of training to ready his or her body for performing the task.

Our vocal folds produce tones through their vibration, but our voice quality is greatly enhanced—and given character, color, and beauty—by the overtones produced as our vocal sounds vibrate throughout the cavities above the vocal folds. Without the added vibration of these spaces within the vocal tract, our vocal sounds would be thin and uninteresting indeed. We need resonance to give richness, amplification, and extension to the original sound. It is the unique resonance of each individual that makes each voice recognizable and interesting, and great artists are known by their distinctive vocal sound. Therefore, the development of an individual's unique sound is a worthy aspiration.

When we speak of the color of a vocal sound, we are actually considering two things: (1) the natural timbre or quality of the voice, which results from the physical structure of the larynx and the resonators—in this case we might speak of the dark, rich color of a voice; and (2) the kinds of sound resulting from some manipulation of these resonators on our part—for example, we might refer to a singer's performance as demonstrating a remarkable change of color, consciously affected to suit the mood of a different character. This latter technique is among the most difficult for a singer to learn to use properly. It has equal importance for an actor or actress, or for anyone who wishes to convey a variety of moods and meanings, or to sway an audience emotionally with his or her voice.

Considering first the natural resonance we desire to bring into our voice, our chief difficulty as beginning students of voice is that—to paraphrase the poet Robert Burns—"no power has given us the giftie to see [hear] ourselves as others see [hear] us." At no time are we able to hear the complete quality of our voice as we are uttering it. We hear not one but two voices: the sound emerging from our mouth and also the sound inside our head. This combination produces a far different effect from the sound that our listeners hear. We hear both inside and outside, so to speak, but never the sound that is transmitted to the far side of the auditorium.

Many of us, having had our voice recorded for the first time, have scarcely recognized ourselves upon hearing the playback. Even the best recording does not sound exactly like the sound we hear in the room or hall where the performance is happening. It is therefore vital that we—as speakers or singers in the initial stages of our development—have someone with taste, understanding, and a technical knowledge of the voice tell us whether or not we are making the most of our phonating apparatus. As we advance, we become used to the sound that our experienced and competent teacher has told us is the best we can make, and we learn to go largely by the feeling we experience—not by listening to ourselves.

Students who haven't learned to do this frequently complain that their newly released voice sounds too "bright" to themselves. This is natural in a beginner first experiencing relaxed and easy voice production and resonance. The sound may seem excessively "brassy" to the speaker or singer, who has become accustomed to making and listening to a vocal sound that probably seemed quite beautiful, though it would not have carried across the room. For the first time, one begins to experience the use of resonance in the right way—and can hardly believe that the voice the listeners hear is merely taking on the clarity, richness, and carrying power that it lacked before. The student must become acquainted with this strange new sound and, above all, get used to the freedom experienced in the throat. Until the ears become attuned, one will almost have to take it on faith from the teacher that these are now the right vocal sounds—recognize that the voice has new-found carrying qualities.

The worst mistake we can make as beginners is to consciously manipulate our sound-making apparatus to imitate vocal qualities and characteristics we admire in others. Each voice is unique. Like fingerprints, there are no two exactly alike—such individuality is, in fact, the chief charm of a voice. We have all known beginning students of voice who listen to a great singer or actor, either in person or by means of recordings, and then try to imitate that person's style and particularly his or her voice quality—perhaps we have even been guilty of this ourselves on occasion! The dangers of such practices, however, should be obvious: we cannot bypass a real understanding of our own limitations and potentialities by trying to appropriate the tone quality of someone with a different anatomy. We must realize that the most important task ahead of us is to express our own vocal personality by allowing the voice to emerge—untrammeled by artificial tensions or manipulations of the articulators before we have achieved a clear understanding of the more fundamental aspects of voice production.

If we concentrate on these fundamentals instead, we will be surprised and delighted to find that the added resonance we did not possess at the start is gradually beginning to enhance the voice and give it better quality and greater size. Resonance will come of its own accord when the relaxation, right breathing, and support already described allow the voice to emerge easily and in a free-flowing manner. One great obstruction to the maintenance of an even resonance or focus throughout the vocal line is mouthing. By this we mean an overuse of jaw action in singing. This serves only to distort vowel sounds and makes it difficult for the singer to articulate consonants in time and with clarity.

We come now to the matter of change of color in the voice. This refers to the practice by which we actually alter the shape of our mouth cavity and pharynx to produce different overtones and thereby different tonal effects. Resonating areas can change or be changed to produce many variations of sound, and thereby to portray a great variety of specific meanings and moods in a song or reading. When an experienced actor gives a reading that involves more than one role, he or she is constantly changing the shape of the vocal tract to produce different effects, clearly indicating to the audience the different characters being portrayed. When an experienced singer performs Schubert's "The Erlking," for example, he must frequently change his voice quality to indicate the four roles—of the Erlking, the father, the son, and the narrator.

By thinking-through these changes, a well-coordinated singer automatically takes on the vocal personalities of different characters—but keep in mind that such a singer is far enough advanced in vocal technique to realize consciously the ways in which to make these changes in color. The singer has already learned to maintain relaxation in the six areas described, and change in the vocal tract is effected with the least possible effort.

It is essential, however, that the student take the advice in this chapter thoroughly to heart before attempting change-of-color techniques. They can be very dangerous if used by a student who has not yet fully understood the difference between the natural voice quality and change of vocal color used for a special effect at a special time. If such manipulation is attempted before the student has gradually and fully developed the natural use of the resonators as part of a program of general vocal development, it will only defeat the purpose. Such refinements cannot be forced; they must come about as the logical and inevitable result of careful study under the watchful guidance of a fine teacher.

Chapter 8

Expressiveness and the McClosky Technique

Janet Alcorn

The wonderful thing about the human voice is its great variety of expression. Your voice mirrors your every feeling. When you call your best friend, doesn't he or she know immediately how you are feeling, just from the sound of your voice?

"Lump in the throat" and "all choked up" are examples of common phrases that describe what can happen when we are reacting to emotion. The problem for the singer/speaker is to be able to convey that emotion without the negative effect upon the voice. In the theater, most acting methods emphasize relaxation and freedom as the necessary beginning point. When freedom is habituated and consistently connected to support and steady breath flow, the whole vocal mechanism responds easily and automatically to thought and emotion. If you are free and you *breathe in the emotion of the phrase,* your voice will mirror that emotion. Let us now look at the idea of expressiveness from the point of view of the areas of relaxation.

The gentle massage of the face (area 1) enables us to identify and eliminate any tensions in the facial muscles. This does not mean we are not going to use these muscles. Tension is the habitual contraction of muscles before they do their work. Freeing the facial muscles means that each muscle group, layer, and individual muscle is available for the widest variety of expressive movement. Freeing the lip muscles means we can form the labial consonants in the most efficient and effective way. (See chapter 5 on articulation.)

The tongue can be thought of in three parts: tip, blade, and root or base. Contraction of the root (area 2) into the swallowing position (area 3) makes it difficult for the blade and tip to properly and efficiently form the shapes and movements of the vowel and consonant sounds. Tension in areas 2 and 3 also limits the color of the voice.

Tension in the jaw (area 4) gives a harsh edge to the tone and limits artic-ulation. A tight jaw tends to look like anger or fear; we can learn to use other facial muscles and body language and the *thought* of those emotions while singing to express them. We can also allow the jaw/neck movements of anger or fear while we are *not* singing and then release them before taking a singing breath. Once the jaw is completely free, the singer can smile and free the jaw at the same time. Thus, he or she can have full resonance and quality of sound and full range of expression.

It is inefficient and unnecessary to use the extrinsic muscles of the neck (area 6) when breathing. This can become an unfortunate habit when one is being "expressive."

The head–neck relationship is the key to the skillful use of the whole body. When the head is easily balanced on the spine, all parts of the vocal tract are in the ideal alignment for full resonance, clear vowels, and efficient diction. The head nod (area 6) enables us to find that balance. Easy balance allows easy movement. The singer can turn, tilt, and move the head however he or she wishes, and then return to balance. Using the head nod in the midst of practicing is most helpful. When you can sing at your loudest, highest, most emotional levels and still have a free neck, you will sound your best *and* be at your most expressive.

In an unconscious effort to "reach their audience," many performers tend to thrust their head forward, leading with the chin. This "emotive pos-ture" is unfortunate, because the muscles at the back of the neck are tight, as is the jaw. The chin is not our most expressive feature—the eyes are.

The following are suggestions to help you discover the full range of emo-tions available to you. A full-length mirror and a hand mirror are valuable tools. When you are changing habitual ways, the new ways can feel "strange" or "wrong." The mirror can reassure you that you do not look as odd as you feel while you are making these changes.

Take any of the exercises in this book and sing them with specific emo-tions—anger, fear, joy, silliness, happiness, tenderness, or passion. Be sure to check the six areas of relaxation and healthy breathing. Treat it as a game. Make up extravagant scenarios (e.g., you just won the lottery, you just heard a very funny joke, your lover just left you, you are comforting a child) Keep changing the emotions. As you think of the emotion and take your breath, the internal changes happen automatically. You will hear and feel the differ-ent emotions in your voice, without adding tension. Find the emotion in the pattern of all your vocal exercises, whether a 5-tone scale or a series of florid patterns. You are always singing with emotion whether you know it or not; often the emotion is, "Oh, I'm so bored," or "Am I on pitch?" An appropriate emotion to start with is, "I Love to Sing!" Florid music in particular needs to be infused with emotion or it becomes mechanical.

Be Specific. Knowing the *general* idea or emotion of a song is not enough. Each phrase has its own emotional content. Look for the changes from one phrase to another. Use a thesaurus to understand the many aspects of one generalized emotion. Keep lists of feelings. Let the poet help you. Look for the color words in each phrase—sometimes a verb (weeping, leaping); sometimes an adverb (sadly, wonderingly); sometimes an adjective (lovely, fierce), and so forth. Let the composer help you. Ask yourself why there is a leap in the phrase, or a descending interval at the end. Listen to the harmonic changes. "Why is that diminished seventh chord there?" "Why is that modulation there?" Pay *specific* attention to all of the composer's markings: "Why is there a diminuendo, ritardando, or accelerando?"

Understand that in a song or aria, the emotions and/or situations are what generate *all* of the music, from the signal before the introduction (*prelude*) through the silence at the end (*after the postlude*). Every note is the singer's responsibility and needs to be understood emotionally, whether it is the spinning wheel turning under Schubert's *Gretchen am Spinnrade,* the fleeing motif in "Pace, Pace Mio Dio," or the sound of longing in the *Tristan* chord.

Once you have a good idea of what the poet and the composer intended, then find the relationship to yourself. How would you express this song in your own words? It can be most illuminating to put an eighteenth-century Italian aria into twenty-first century American slang.

Whether singing or speaking, we must convey human emotions in order to effectively communicate. All voice users can benefit from incorporating the McClosky Technique for expression as well as voice production.

The great Irish tenor, John McCormack, had the right idea when he said, "Keep a cool head and a warm heart." You will feel comfortable and your audience will respond. You will be demonstrating "the art which conceals the art," which is to make performance seem easy and natural, and you will establish a real rapport with your audience. Freedom and expression combine for a powerful result.

Chapter 9

Care of the Voice

Bonnie Pomfret

For optimum voice use, good health is of vital importance; in a sense, all voice users, whether their primary activity is speaking or singing, are vocal athletes. If we consider that the average rate of vocal fold vibration for speech is around 100 Hz (cycles or vibrations per second) for an adult male, and around 200 Hz for an adult female (and that the range for singers is from about 50 to over 1000 Hz), we can only wonder at our ability to use our voices hour after hour on a daily basis. Each of us is occasionally aware of the voice's vulnerabilities: even a slight cold or allergy can adversely affect vocal function, and many other factors in the body can influence the voice for better or worse. Yet, with good care, the voice can function quite well into advanced age.

In this chapter you will find a few recommendations for general health and fitness and then an examination of the most important issues for maintaining vocal health including: hydration, or water level in the body, with a discussion on substances that have a drying effect; common health problems such as gastro-esophageal reflux disease and colds; some classes of medication that have been shown to have an adverse effect on the voice; and some general recommendations for healthy voice use. These are general comments, intended as guidelines, and we recommend that the reader consult a qualified health professional for any individual question or problem.

General Health

General health and fitness are important for the singer and speaker. The body will respond better to any demand made upon it, if it is rested, well-nourished, and reasonably fit. We urge our readers to think of themselves as "vocal athletes" and treat their bodies accordingly. The foundation for vocal health is built on three factors: sleep, diet, and exercise.

Adequate sleep is very important to the voice user. Singers especially need rest. Remember that the body repairs and rebuilds during sleep. The recommended amount of sleep for the average adult is eight hours per night, although studies indicate that adults are getting less sleep than ever. If you would like to know how much sleep you need, the next time you have a vacation, try going to bed at the same time every night and not setting an alarm. After about 10 days, you will begin to awaken at the same time; this is probably a fair indication of how much sleep you need. You will also notice a feeling of well-being and increased energy.

Diet is a topic of considerable concern in our modern society, and even in the research community there is much controversy about what constitutes a healthy diet. Each individual should find a sensible and nutritious diet that promotes a healthy weight and provides the necessary nutrition for a sense of well-being. It seems safe to say that most Americans would benefit from an increase in fresh fruits and vegetables, and a decrease in refined carbohydrates and fatty foods including red meat. Detailed dietary recommendations are beyond the scope of this volume.

While the cliché of the overweight singer lingers in popular culture, research has shown that fitness is very important for all voice users. As Dr. Robert T. Sataloff writes:

> A singer whose respiratory and abdominal conditioning is not good enough to allow him or her to walk up a few flights of stairs without becoming winded probably is unable to maintain good abdominal support throughout a recital or opera. When the power source of the voice is undermined in this way, excessive muscle use in the neck and tongue usually supervenes.[1]

Our recommendation is that each person develop a fitness regime appropriate to body type and age that helps to improve and maintain aerobic capacity, strength, and flexibility. Remember that as we age, muscle mass is lost, and for a voice user this could have serious consequences on posture, breathing, and support. Before beginning any program of physical exercise, consult your physician.

Think of a healthy lifestyle as an investment in the quality of your life and in promoting longevity. If you invest wisely and well, you will reap benefits in the years to come. As we age, the habits of a lifetime may be revealed in the condition of the voice; if health habits are bad, the voice can suffer prematurely; if health habits are good, the voice can continue to function with little deterioration, even into advanced age.

Special Health Considerations for Voice Users

Now we come to special considerations for voice users. The first is water, and it is of vital importance. The vocal folds are a small part of the upper respiratory tract, which extends from the mouth and nose down through the lungs. This tract is lined with the mucous membrane or mucous blanket, which has several functions; generally speaking, it serves as a moist layer to trap and remove unwanted inhaled particles and to provide a layer of protection over the tissue that it covers.

When we are healthy, the mucous membrane produces about a liter daily of clear, thin, watery mucus. Even though the nose is producing mucus, we are unaware of it and swallow it without noticing. However, if we are ill, breathe in polluted air, or force the vocal folds together too forcefully, the membrane begins to produce additional mucus to protect the tissue beneath. We have the sensation of needing to clear the throat or blow the nose.

The first and most important way to keep the mucous membrane functioning well is to drink water, approximately eight glasses per day. It is not necessary to buy bottled water; any water that is safe to drink will serve the purpose. Other liquids may or may not be equivalent to water; see comments below. To quote Van Lawrence, MD, in four most useful words for voice users: "Sing wet; pee pale."

To check if you are getting enough water, there is a simple guide; the color of your urine. If it is pale, you are probably well hydrated; if it is bright yellow, you probably need to drink more water. It should be noted that some vitamin supplements can cause bright color of the urine. Minimize or avoid diuretics, such as caffeine, alcohol, cold medications, and antihistamines; they draw water from your system as they are metabolized and have an overall drying effect.

The amount of water in the air is also a consideration for the voice user. We lose a little water vapor every time we exhale. In spaces where heating and air conditioning are required, the relative humidity is generally lower, and especially at night, when we do not drink water for some hours, we may find ourselves feeling parched upon awakening. If this is the case, you may benefit from using a humidifier. It is important to keep a humidifier clean and to keep humidity at moderate levels, to avoid the growth of bacteria and molds, which can cause problems as well.

Sometimes you do not have control over the environment, such as when traveling, speaking, or performing in a new space. If traveling and feeling dry, one of the first things to do when you check into a hotel is to run hot water in the shower and allow the steam to enter the room. In a place where you perform or speak, you may have to resort to some of our "quick fixes."

Quick fixes that help restore moisture to the mucous membrane are breathing steam and nasal lavage. Each of these methods helps relieve nasal congestion or dryness by bringing moisture directly to the mucous membrane in the nose and upper respiratory tract. To breathe steam, you can simply fill a sink with hot water from the tap, bend over the sink, and make a small tent out of a towel to trap the steam. Breathe this steam for a few minutes. Portable facial steamers are also available.

Nasal lavage (or irrigation) literally rinses the nasal passages with salt water, helping the mucous membrane in its function of waste removal. It is an ancient practice in India, and singers have sworn by it for centuries; recent research has shown that nasal lavage reduces the incidence of sinus infections. Mix one cup of lukewarm water and ½ teaspoon salt. This solution can be sniffed, sprayed, or inhaled into the nose, or, using a Neti pot, poured into one nostril at a time. Do not save any leftover solution and be sure any vessel is thoroughly cleaned between uses.

Colds

The "common cold," is caused by not one but a number of different viruses. Since colds are viral in origin, there is no cure other than the body's own rest. First and foremost, the best way to avoid colds is to wash your hands frequently and keep your body's defenses up through good health habits. However, nearly everyone succumbs to an upper respiratory infection from time to time, and voice use can be significantly compromised by mucus and swelling in the vocal tract.

The many cold medications available on the market provide relief from symptoms but do not cure the cold; most medications have multiple ingredients, which can be confusing. In fact, in the section of this chapter that deals with medications that can have an adverse effect on the voice, you will find many of these ingredients in cold medicines. The issue is thorny: is it better to use medicines to be rid of a symptom or symptoms in order to try and function normally, using the vocal folds when they are impaired, or is it better to "ride it out," rest, take none but the most innocuous medicines, and give the body a chance for its own healing? While we would generally recommend the latter, we leave each reader to answer this question for him- or herself, depending on the situation. Be forewarned, however, that many of the singers who end up at the doctor's office were doing fine until they tried to continue their usual schedule while suffering from a cold or secondary infection. You would not run a road race on a sprained ankle.

First, be sure to get additional fluids to keep the mucus thin and moving, reducing congestion, coughing, and inflammation. Guaifenesin, an ingredient found in the simplest cough medicines as well as in pill form, does a good job at keeping the mucus thin.

Second, rest the voice and the body as much as possible. If you are a professional voice user, this is the time to utilize an alternate plan that minimizes your voice use, for example catching up on paperwork, showing a film to a class, doing mental work such as memorization, etc.

Third, remember that a cold must run its course, but that it also weakens the body and renders it susceptible to secondary infections such as sinusitis, bronchitis, etc. If you suspect that your cold is turning into something else, or if symptoms recur, it is time to see your health care provider.

GERD

Gastroesophageal reflux disease, known as "GERD" or "reflux," is very common among professional voice users. In this disorder, partially digested foods (which contain a great deal of acid from the digestive tract) come back up the esophagus as a result of the failure of a valve at the top of the stomach. In laryngo-phrayngeal reflux, known as "LPR," the spillage continues up into the larynx. Chapter 10 on voice disorders provides further information. Certain foods (mostly spicy or acidic) seem to aggravate this condition.

There are several approaches to treating GERD. The most conservative would include a reduction in the size of meals, avoidance of eating at least three hours before lying down, avoidance of "trigger" foods if they can be identified, raising the head of the bed about six inches, and use of antacids. A more aggressive approach would be daily or twice daily medication; although this type of medication is available over the counter, a diagnosis from a physician should come first. The most aggressive approach is surgery to repair the faulty valve.

An important point for voice users is that hoarseness of the type we call "morning voice" is not considered normal but may indeed be an indicator of reflux. Post-performance eating, as well as overconsumption of coffee, alcohol, and spicy foods, can contribute to this condition.

Allergies and Asthma

Allergies are a complex topic, but a short definition of allergy might be: an abnormal response to contact with a normal substance. In voice users, the "histamine response" of allergy can cause swelling of the mucous membranes, overproduction of mucus, sneezing, coughing, and other reactions, all of which compromise phonation. Many allergy medications, traditionally anti-histamines, cause dryness and some can cause drowsiness. Some recent therapies target other parts of the allergic response and have shown promise. In youngsters or young adults, desensitization can give virtually permanent relief. Consult your health care professional.

Asthma, a chronic lung disorder that is marked by recurring episodes of airway obstruction with labored breathing, wheezing, and coughing, triggered by hyper-reactivity to various stimuli (as allergens or rapid change in air temperature), can have devastating effects on voice use. There are many voice professionals who suffer from asthma who, with proper care and treatment, function quite well. Finding the right medication and dosage may take patience and persistence.

Many questions arise as to whether professional voice users should avoid dairy products, chocolate, or other specific foods. There is not a general answer; any of these substances may be an issue for one individual and not for another. True food allergy is rare and usually serious enough that voice quality is not the primary consideration. Reactions to such substances would

probably be classified as food sensitivities, rather than allergies, and avoidance of the culprit is usually enough to solve the problem. Dairy products can
cause overproduction of mucus in some individuals, and these individuals
should be aware of that effect on the voice and avoid them before speaking or
singing engagements. Others have no difficulty. Chocolate contains small
amounts of caffeine, but what seems to bother some voice users is another of
its ingredients: lecithin. Lecithin is made from soy and used in many foods,
providing a smooth or creamy texture. Some people react adversely to it by
producing too much mucus.

Medications

Voice users should remember that for the voice to function at its best, the
fine coordination required for vocal communication depends on a number of
factors. We have discussed the issue of hydration, which is of primary importance for the mucous blanket.

Now we come to issues for those who take medications for other medical
problems. This chapter can provide only general information on medications
that have been demonstrated to have an adverse effect on the voice; the voice
user who is aware of potential problems can work with health care providers
to find the best overall solution. Remember also that herbal remedies and
homeopathic medicines, while popular, are not closely regulated or
researched in the United States.

Vocal efficiency is dependent on adequate hydration. In addition to our
discussion of hydration in general, it is important to know that there are a
number of common medications that change the fluid balance in the body:
diuretics, used for the treatment of hypertension and kidney problems;
decongestants, used in cold and allergy medications; antispasmodics, used
for treatment of diarrhea; antitussives, used in cough medicines; some acne
medications; and some antipsychotic medicines.

Coordination can be affected by stimulants, depressants, and anesthetics.
Stimulants are found in caffeine, nicotine, amphetamines, diet aids, and cold
preparations. Depressants are found in alcohol and tranquilizers. Anesthetics
are found in throat lozenges and throat sprays.

Increased risk of vocal fold hemorrhage has been associated with some
pain relief medications in conjunction with strenuous voice use (see chapter
10 for more information). Aspirin and the nonsteroidal anti-inflammatory
drugs (NSAIDs), such as ibuprofen, naproxen, ketaprofen, and many others,
are the chief concerns. Only one type of pain reliever, acetaminophen, has not
been shown to increase risk of vocal fold hemorrhage. Consult your health
care professional if you are taking aspirin or NSAIDs for medical conditions.

Agents Causing Structural Changes

Androgens (male hormones), used for hormonal problems in meno-
pausal women, have been shown to cause permanent virilization (lowered

range) in the female voice. Hormones administered in birth-control pills can also have an effect upon the voice; consult your health professional to find the best choice for you.

We cannot proceed to the next section without mentioning smoking. Smoking causes cancer, and secondary smoke is devastating to the vocal tract. If you are serious about your voice and your health, avoid smoking and smoky environments.

Healthy Voice Habits

Daily habits can also have an effect on the functioning of the voice. We have a few suggestions for the voice user. First let us look at some habits that can detract from optimum voice function. These are activities to avoid:

1. Shouting, screaming, raucous laughter, and extended loud talking (i.e., voice strain that often occurs at sporting events, parties, loud restaurants)

2. Long conversations in trains, planes, or cars where you have to twist the neck or head

3. Speaking or singing above loud noises such as traffic, loud parties, stereos, or television

4. Excessive throat clearing and coughing

5. Breathing smoke, dust, and fumes

6. Glottal attacks for emphasis

7. Vocal fry

8. Talking in awkward positions when on the phone

9. Overly loud speaking on the phone, especially cell phones in noisy surroundings

10. Singing when breathing is compromised (by abdominal cramping, congestion, or pregnancy)

11. Unnecessary use of decongestants and antihistamines before presentations or performances

12. Alcohol and elective medications before presentations or performances

13. Prolonged singing at either extreme of range or dynamics

14. Smoking *anything!* And secondary smoke

15. Exercise that elicits the Valsalva response (weight lifting, upper-body building, tennis)

16. Practicing or performing when the voice is raspy or rough for whatever reason—the show does *not* have to go on!

Here are some suggestions for how to maintain your voice by using it sensibly:

1. "Warm up" your voice first thing in the morning. Take deep breaths, do tongue stretches and gentle humming.
2. Practice a few minutes at a time—several times a day.
3. Drink plenty of water.
4. Speak in a moderate speaking tone—neither too loud nor too soft.
5. Avoid sudden increases in voice use (long presentations, rehearsals or performances)—build up gradually.
6. Be aware of everyday stresses that can cause tension in the vocal mechanism.
7. Sing literature or choral parts in your correct range.
8. Take frequent breaks. This is especially important for young voices.
9. In speaking, vary your tone, inflection, and volume.
10. If you need to call a group to attention, use hand clapping or flicker a light switch rather than using your voice.
11. If ill, take it easy and let your body recuperate through rest.

Conclusions

The voice user will benefit from a healthy lifestyle and adequate hydration; a healthy voice resides in a healthy body. If illness strikes, medications should be taken with the awareness that they may have an adverse effect on the voice. Women should be aware of possible effects of any hormones they take. Anyone experiencing voice problems should work with a physician to find the best solution.

Daily warm-up and practice routines will keep your voice ready for use. Good technique becomes more important as you place more demands on your voice, and as you age. Voice conservation, especially in noisy environments, is advised. With good care, your voice should perform well for a lifetime!

Note

[1] Robert T. Sataloff, *Vocal Health and Pedagogy*, first edition (San Diego: Singular Publishing Group, 1998), 129.

Chapter 10

Voice Disorders

Bonnie Pomfret

$\mathcal{S}$ince David Blair McClosky wrote *Your Voice at Its Best* in the late 1950s, medical technology has provided new tools for observing the larynx—namely, the fiber-optic laryngoscope and videostroboscopy. With the former, a close view of the vocal folds is possible; with the latter, fine movements of the folds can be observed. These innovations, now in general use by otolaryngologists and speech pathologists, have yielded a new understanding of the function of the vocal folds, as well as better diagnosis and treatment of voice disorders. This chapter has been updated to include recent developments and terminology. In the 1950s McClosky believed that muscle tension played a significant role in voice disorders—and in recent years the term Muscle Tension Dysphonia has come into use. Although muscle tension seems to be a component in many voice disorders, its exact role has yet to be determined.

In its normal state, the larynx is a marvelous mechanism, capable of hundreds of movements per second as well as all the other adjustments necessary for speech and singing. In the vast majority of individuals, the voice functions without injury throughout the life span; we rely on the voice and assume it will meet all our demands. In some activities for which the voice is used vigorously in volume or duration, such as acting, teaching, singing, or sales work, training and good technique can help condition the voice to meet the greater challenges. Those who pursue such vocally rigorous activities should seek training for their voice and be aware of the physical demands on their voice. Each individual may have a different ability to use the voice vigorously, but just as in any sport, training can improve function.

Changes in the body, or in the way the voice is used, can cause undesirable changes in the voice, which, if they continue unchecked, can cause voice disorders. In this chapter we will provide an overview of the principal voice disorders. Many disorders involve changes in the tissue of the vocal folds as a result of repeated mechanical stress to the vocal folds themselves; these changes take several different forms. Some voice disorders involve the body's reaction to irritants; others are a result of muscle weakness or imbalance. The causes of several disorders are still unknown as of this writing.

Once there is a change in the voice—no matter what its cause—the individual tries to adapt to the problem. These efforts may be subtle, and they may not be conscious. In the initial phases, many disorders cause more effortful production of voice and result in compensatory straining or overuse of the muscles. When this "extra effort" becomes a habit, it becomes a secondary element of—and may actually contribute to—the disorder. When the time comes for treatment, therefore, the majority of voice disorders have a muscle tension component, which should be addressed. The McClosky Technique, with its emphasis on easy-onset phonation and breath coordination, offers help in dealing with muscle tension related to voice use.

Common Disorders of the Voice

The most common disorder of the voice consists of redness, roughness, or swelling (edema) of the vocal folds and is usually called *laryngitis*, characterized by varying degrees of hoarseness, huskiness, and general fatigue of the throat after sustained speaking or singing. *Acute laryngitis* generally results from infection or sudden trauma. *Chronic laryngitis* is more likely to be a consequence of vocal overuse or misuse and can be associated with other trauma to the vocal folds, such as that of reflux.

Let us digress a moment here to speak of water levels in the body (i.e., hydration), which can play a role in laryngitis. The lining of the vocal and respiratory tract is covered with mucous membrane, which—when healthy and supplied with enough water—produces clear, watery mucus. We are unconscious of its existence when we are well—and well-hydrated. Research has shown that hydration clearly affects vocal performance; tests on singers in the 1980s showed that several important aspects of vocal production were better when the singer was well-hydrated than when the same singer was dehydrated.

Why should this be so? When the body's water balance is disturbed—for example, through an infection, through excessive use of caffeine or alcohol, or through use of medications that cause a drying effect (diuretic)—the mucus becomes thick. Rather than providing a thin layer of lubrication, thick drops or strands of mucus cling to areas of the vocal tract, including the vocal folds. The individual may have a feeling of dryness, a need to clear the throat frequently, or a feeling that it just "takes more work" to get the voice moving. Some voice professionals have named this condition *laryngitis sicca* (literally, inflamed dry larynx). In addition, the gelatinous layer that is a chief component of the vibrating part of the vocal fold reacts to the levels of water in the body and it moves better when we are well hydrated.

We now come to the more serious cases of vocal abuse, resulting in benign (nonmalignant) growths on the folds:

- The most common growth is a *nodule*, sometimes called "singer's node." These callous-like protuberances occur in pairs—opposite each other on the folds, usually at the junction of the anterior and middle thirds, where the greatest vibration occurs in phonation. The folds, instead of meeting precisely, irritate each other by touching too forcefully at this point, until, after a while, the nodules develop, much as a corn or callous may develop on the toe from a too-tight shoe. The growth is easily resolved by vocal retraining unless it is of long standing and has become especially fibrous.

- *Polyps* are another form of benign growth, which are often treated successfully by voice therapy and/or surgery. They may take the form of a growth along the edge of the fold or beneath it, or there may be a single protuberance emerging from the fold on a tiny stem. There is some difference of opinion among otolaryngologists as to the exact cause of polyps; trauma may be a factor, as well as alcohol and smoking. It seems evident from the cases that have responded to therapy that vocal abuse is a factor in their formation and recurrence after surgical removal.

- *Cysts* may occur on the vocal folds. They are usually fluid-filled and have been described as resembling the consistency of a grape. It is believed that the cyst is a result of trauma in which a mucous gland duct is blocked, but other causes are possible. Sometimes the cyst causes swelling, or even a nodule-like swelling to appear on the opposite fold; sometimes this becomes clear when only one side resolves with voice therapy. Surgery is usually performed on cysts and postoperative therapy is recommended.

- *Vocal-fold hemorrhage* seems to be associated with a violent use of the voice (such as screaming or singing while ill) or with physical trauma to the larynx. In this disorder, small blood vessels within the vocal fold rupture, allowing blood to spill out into the surrounding tissue. This can be seen as a dark or "bruised" area on the folds. The event causes immediate, severe hoarseness or loss of voice, which does not abate. The use of aspirin and other blood-thinning medications increases the risk of vocal fold hemorrhage. The usual treatment for a hemorrhage is total voice rest, allowing the blood to be reabsorbed into the body; this may take several weeks. Vocal retraining may be in order.

- *Reinke's edema* is the breakdown and swelling of an entire layer below the surface of the vocal fold. This layer, known as Reinke's Space, is comprised of tissue of a gelatinous consistency, which allows the vocal folds to vibrate in response to air flowing between them. The characteristic of Reinke's edema is swelling along the entire length of the vocal fold, giving a "floppy" appearance when movement is observed. This disorder seems to occur most frequently in people who are heavy smokers. Their speaking pitch is very low, and the voice of a woman with this disorder might be mistaken for that of a man. Treatment includes surgery and voice therapy.

- *Gastro-esophageal reflux disease* (GERD) can cause problems for the voice in the form of *laryngo-pharyngeal reflux* (LPR). Both of these disorders are commonly referred to as "reflux." In GERD, due to a failure of a sphincter mechanism at the top of the stomach, partially digested food and acids from the digestive tract come back up the esophagus; in LPR, it spills over into the larynx. This condition can occur at any time, but most frequently it happens at night when the patient is lying down, and the posterior portion of the larynx, including the vocal folds, becomes red and irritated from the contact with these stomach acids. The voice is hoarse in the morning and, unlike most disorders, which worsen with voice use, generally improves throughout the day.

  Those who suffer from "morning voice" should be aware that "reflux," could be the cause. Caffeine, alcohol, and spicy foods seem to be the chief contributors; but singers seem to be particularly prone to the problem, and that may be related to the abdominal action of breathing for singing. GERD seems to be a widespread problem, and is frequently treated by otolaryngologists with acid-reducing medications and/or lifestyle adjustments such as changes in diet, raising the head of the bed, and avoidance of late-night eating.

- *Granuloma* occurs as a response to trauma, usually after a breathing tube has been inserted between the vocal folds during surgery. The tissue that forms at the site of the trauma is granular. Treatment includes surgical removal and voice therapy.

- *Contact ulcers of the larynx* generally occur on one or both of the folds, at the vocal process where the fold is attached at the back. GERD seems to be a contributing factor. Contact ulcers respond to medical treatment for the GERD and voice therapy.

- *Papilloma* is caused by the human papilloma virus (HPV), which causes growths along the vocal folds that disturb the vibratory edge. Since this is a viral infection, there is no cure. Surgical removal of the diseased tissue can be performed when the growths become large. This is followed by some period with reduced symptoms, but the growths recur.

Two disorders of a different sort are characterized by the fact that the vocal folds, rather than meeting too strongly, are unable to meet. The more common of the two complaints is *vocal fold atrophy*; the more serious disorder is *vocal fold immobility*, which includes paralysis and paresis.

- *Vocal fold atrophy,* also known as *presbyphonia,* tends to occur in older individuals. As in the rest of the body, muscle mass reduces with age. The edges of the folds, which are composed of several layers of muscular tissue, lose bulk, and instead of remaining straight, they curve concavely and cannot meet. Too much air is thus allowed to pass between them, resulting in a chronically breathy (but effortful) hoarseness. While some physicians inject substances into the vocal folds to add bulk, therapy can often improve the condition.

- In *vocal fold paresis* (some loss of movement) and *paralysis* (total loss of movement), one or both folds cannot function fully through loss of movement from injury or disease. Surgical thyroplasty can offer relief by the insertion of material into one or both vocal folds to allow them to meet. Therapy is also successful; so long as there is the possibility of innervation in either vocal fold, it is possible to give the patient a better voice through strengthening those muscles that are still able to function.

Rare Disorders of the Voice

Now we shall look at some rarer disorders whose causes are not fully known.

- *Spasmodic dysphonia* is a disorder in which the vocal folds exhibit sudden opening or closing in a spasm-like movement, causing intermittent disruption of the sound in speech. Its cause is unknown. At the time of this writing, the most effective treatment is the injection of botulism toxin into one or both folds, causing a lessening of the uncontrolled movement on that side. With the correct dosage, this treatment is effective in most cases and lasts about three months, when it must be repeated. In some cases, voice therapy has been helpful.

- *Ventricular phonation* is a disorder in which the patient uses the false vocal folds (ventricular bands) for phonation, along with, or instead of, the true folds. In many cases the false folds function so readily that it is very difficult even to see between them to catch a glimpse of the true folds. In this case the voice sounds extremely hoarse and may have a gravelly or breathy quality, though effortful. Voice therapy is the usual treatment.

- *Aphonia* is the absence of voice. The larynx appears normal, but the vocal folds do not function properly for phonation. Usually the folds are able to meet for coughing or throat clearing. Aphonia appears after trauma of a physical or psychological nature. Voice therapy is the usual treatment.

- *Mutational dysphonia* is a childlike voice quality retained past puberty. While the laryngeal apparatus has matured, the voice use has not. Voice therapy is the usual treatment, and it usually provides rapid relief.

Note to Singers: The fine adjustments necessary for singing require the vocal apparatus to be in excellent condition. Singers have the reputation of being overly worried about their vocal condition, but they are much more attuned to small changes than the layperson. Many singers suffering from problems notice changes long before a disorder can be observed. As technological improvements allow ever better imaging of the larynx in conditions where normal vocal tasks can be performed and observed, our understanding of these minute changes will increase.

Appendix A

Illustrations of the Anatomy and Physiology of the Vocal Mechanism

James Scott Fuller

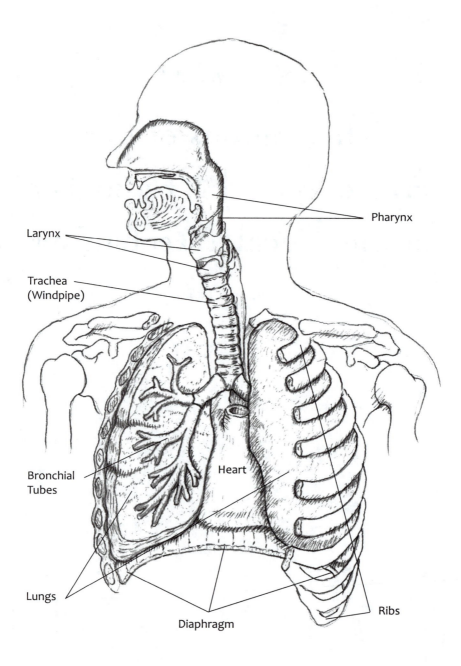

Figure 1: Vocal Mechanism

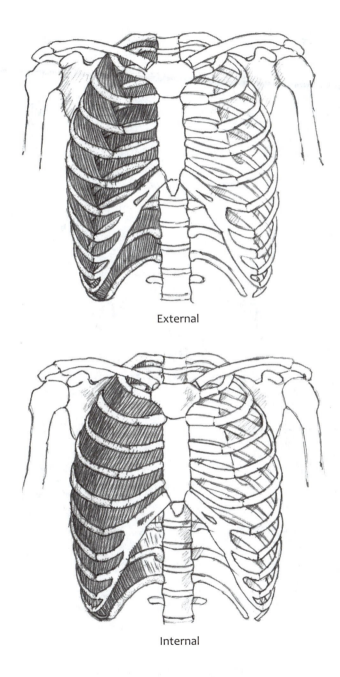

External

Internal

Figure 2: Intercostal Muscles

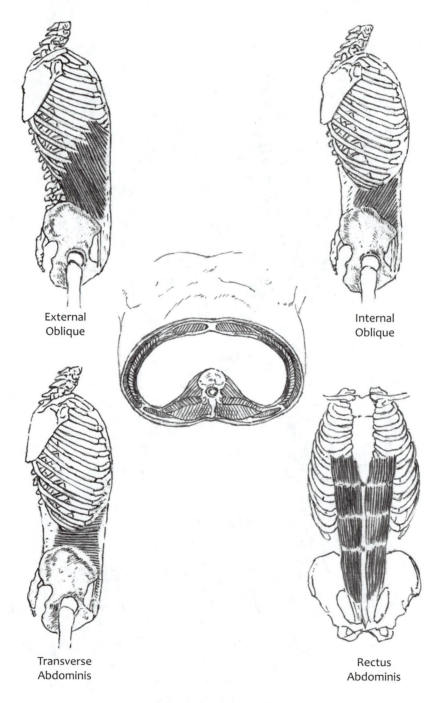

External
Oblique

Internal
Oblique

Transverse
Abdominis

Rectus
Abdominis

Figure 3: Abdominal Muscles
The abdomen is a complete cylinder.

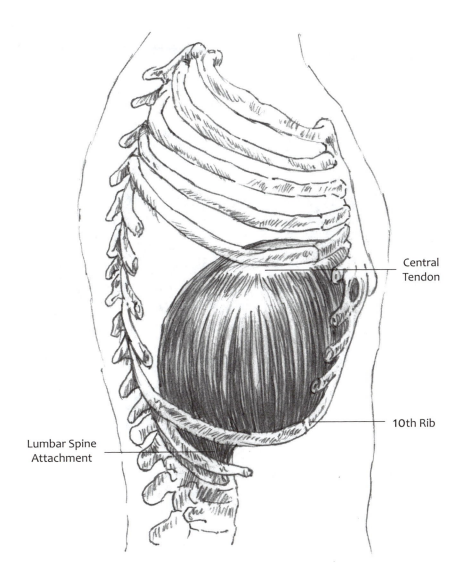

Central
Tendon

10th Rib

Lumbar Spine
Attachment

Figure 4: Diaphragm

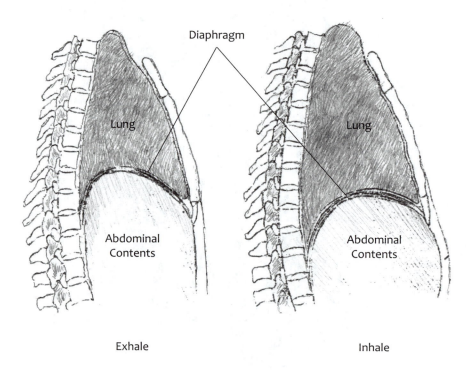

Diaphragm

Lung

Lung

Abdominal
Contents

Abdominal
Contents

Exhale

Inhale

Figure 5: Action of the Diaphragm

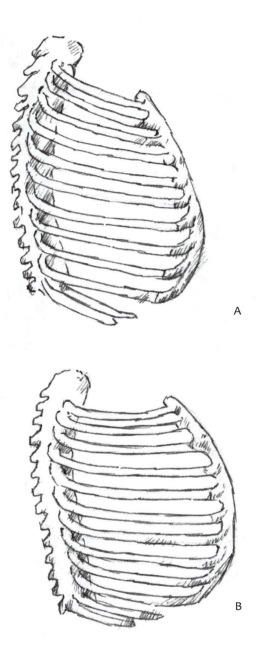

Figure 6: Ribs in Repose (A) and in Position for Phonation (B)

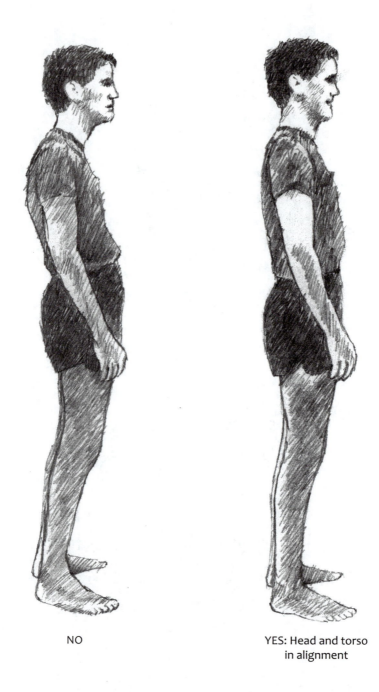

NO   YES: Head and torso
                                          in alignment

Figure 7: Standing Posture

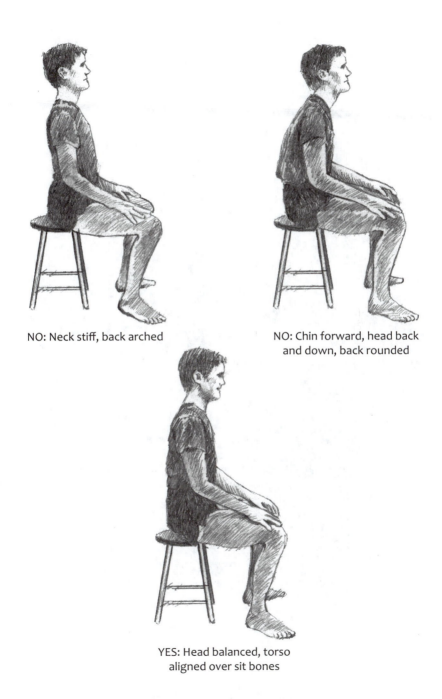

NO: Neck stiff, back arched

NO: Chin forward, head back and down, back rounded

YES: Head balanced, torso aligned over sit bones

Figure 8: Sitting Posture

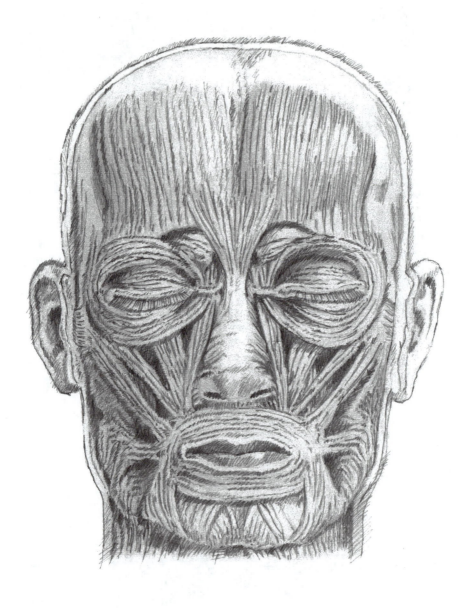

Figure 9: Relaxation Area 1
Muscles of the Face

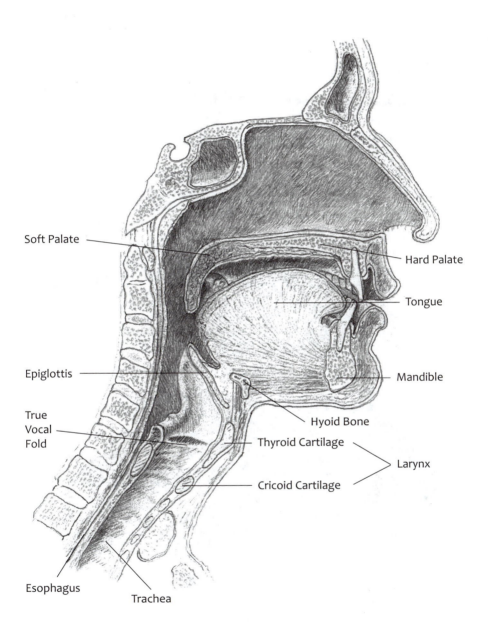

Soft Palate

Hard Palate

Tongue

Epiglottis

Mandible

True
Vocal
Fold

Hyoid Bone

Thyroid Cartilage

Larynx

Cricoid Cartilage

Esophagus

Trachea

Figure 10: Relaxation Area 2
Tongue

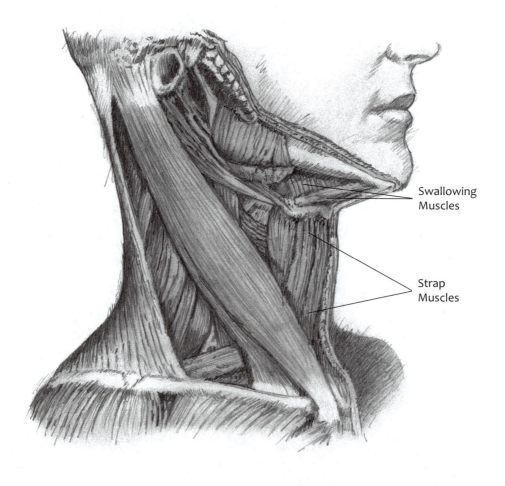

Figure 11: Relaxation Areas 3 and 5
Swallowing and Strap Muscles

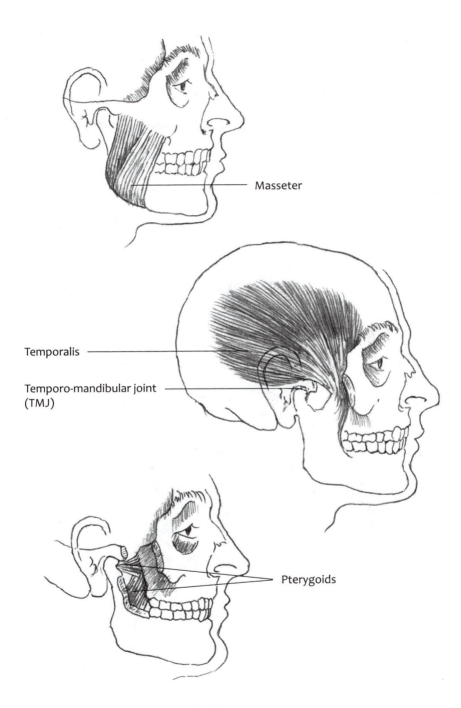

**Figure 12: Relaxation Area 4
Muscles that Close the Jaw**

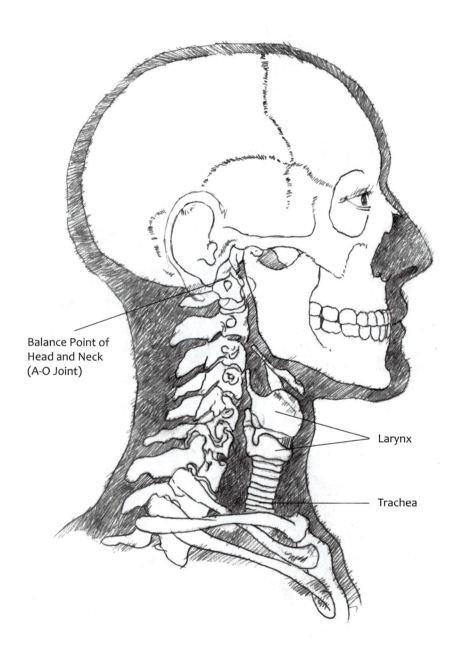

Balance Point of
Head and Neck
(A-O Joint)

Larynx

Trachea

Figure 13: Relaxation Area 6
Balance of the Head and Neck

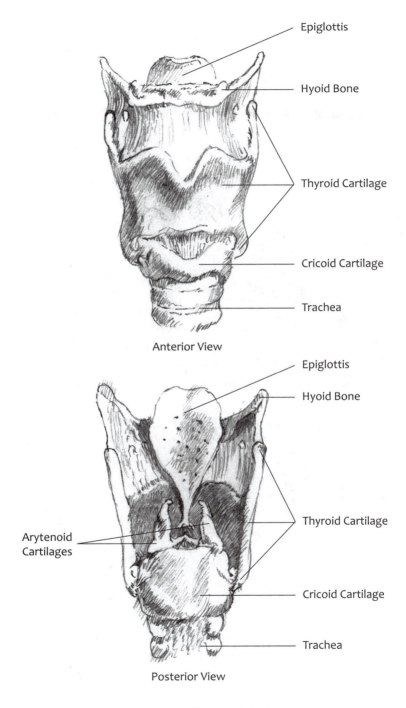

Anterior View

Posterior View

Figure 14: Cartilages of the Larynx

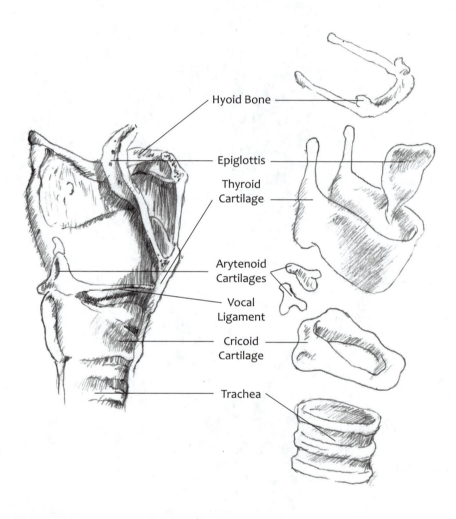

Hyoid Bone

Epiglottis

Thyroid
Cartilage

Arytenoid
Cartilages

Vocal
Ligament

Cricoid
Cartilage

Trachea

Figure 15: Parts of the Larynx, Lateral View

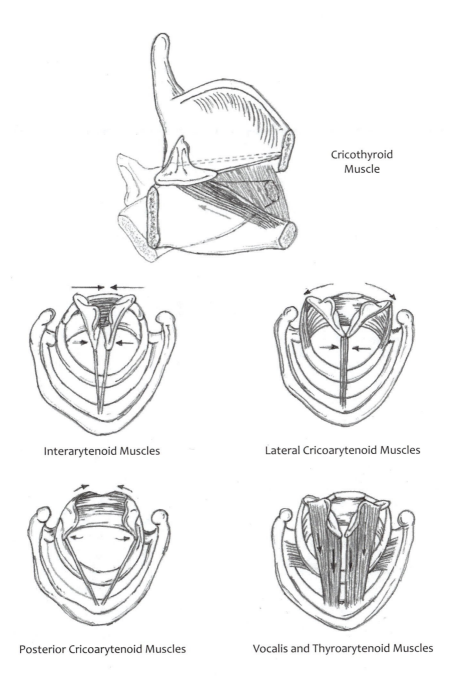

Cricothyroid Muscle

Interarytenoid Muscles

Lateral Cricoarytenoid Muscles

Posterior Cricoarytenoid Muscles

Vocalis and Thyroarytenoid Muscles

Figure 16: Action of Intrinsic Muscles of the Larynx

Appendix B

Biography of
David Blair McClosky

 n David Blair McClosky's 70 years of dedication to the vocal arts, he studied them from every conceivable angle. Born in 1902 in Oswego, New York, to musical parents—they both were professional singers and teachers of singing—he spent many years as a concert and opera singer himself. His first professional engagement was at the age of 17, and he began teaching while still in high school. He studied for six years at the New England Conservatory of Music and did his post-graduate study in Berlin and Milan.

In 1923 he became Boston's first radio announcer, on WNAC. He stayed until 1924. He made more than 20 appearances as soloist with the Boston Symphony and sang with many of the country's other major symphony orchestras. He appeared as a soloist in several Bach festivals and gave five recitals in New York's Town Hall—as well as in Boston's Jordan Hall and in Milan, Berlin, Nigeria, and Ghana. He was a member of the Chicago Opera Company and spent two seasons in light opera. During World War II he served as an Army officer, performing public relations duties in the United States and Africa.

He taught music or voice at Syracuse University, Boston University, Boston Conservatory of Music, the New England Conservatory, Phillips Academy, Andover, and Bradford College. He was a consultant at various times to numerous other universities. From 1946 to 1955, he was Director of the Plymouth Rock Center of Music and Drama, which became widely known for its excellence in furthering the careers of young professional singers, instrumentalists, dancers, and drama and art students.

In 1946, he became interested in voice therapy and, for five years, worked with Dr. Irl Blaisdell of Syracuse, studying both singers and patients with functional voice disorders. From 1952 to 1965, assisted by his wife Barbara,

85

he worked as Clinical Voice Therapist at the Massachusetts Eye and Ear Infirmary and treated private patients from all over the country and abroad. During the same period he developed a course in voice therapy for graduate students at Boston University, where he served on the faculty.

He was vocal advisor to the late President John F. Kennedy. Dave Powers and Kenneth O'Donnell, White House aides to President Kennedy, first disclosed Mr. McClosky's contribution to the 1960 campaign in the book, *Johnny We Hardly Knew Ye.* "It was a great secret," Powers said in a 1984 interview. He recalled how "Mr. McClosky's advice to all comers . . . is to relax, maintain good posture, breathe deeply, and reduce any tightness in the neck." Other beneficiaries of his expertise included President Lyndon B. Johnson; Gov. Michael S. Dukakis; actors Faye Dunaway, Al Pacino, Jill Clayburgh, and Ruth Gordon; and folksinger Joan Baez. McClosky was also adviser to governors Endicott Peabody of Massachusetts and Kenneth Curtis of Maine, and sportscaster Curt Gowdy, as well as many other politicians and public personalities.

In 1967, McClosky retired from Boston University and immediately joined the faculty of the Boston Conservatory, where he established another graduate course in voice therapy. In 1976, Dr. William Montgomery and Dr. Robert Lofgren of Massachusetts Eye and Ear Infirmary were instrumental in re-establishing the voice therapy clinic, which ran until 1983, using the McClosky Technique.

McClosky was author of *Your Voice at Its Best*, and co-authored *Voice in Song and Speech* with his wife, Barbara McClosky. In 1980 Gov. Edward J. King—whose voice Mr. McClosky had once likened to that of a truck driver—named McClosky to a term on the Massachusetts Council on the Arts and Humanities.

At age 79 he was baritone soloist in the Verdi *Requiem,* and at 80, he gave a solo recital. McClosky taught until his final illness in 1988.

David Fairchild Remembers Blair McClosky

I met David Blair McClosky in 1947 at Syracuse University, where he was teaching voice at the time. He soon persuaded me that I really should be in the music program as a voice major. So with his help and guidance, I continued at Syracuse for another three years, and received my music degree.

During the years I was with "Mac," as I knew him, one of the many important and influential things that he and his wife Barbara did was to run a summer opera camp based in Plymouth, Massachusetts. I went to the camp for three summers, and they were the greatest summers of my life. Students attending the camp came from Syracuse and from other colleges and universities all over the country. The camp provided us with the opportunity to learn and perform complete operatic roles in fully staged productions with orchestra. (The orchestra was made up of music students from Baldwin Wallace College in Ohio, under the direction of George Poinar, a faculty member from the college.) Professional singers, directors, and coaches were there to work with the students, and even perform with them.

In 1950, my last summer there, Hans Busch from Indiana University was there to direct all of the operas. That fall he went to the Metropolitan Opera to stage new productions of *Cavalleria Rusticana* and *I Pagliacci*. Ellen Faull was brought in to sing Donna Anna—a role she was already singing with the New York City Opera—in that summer's production of *Don Giovanni*. Benjamin DeLoache, a professional bass who taught voice for many years at Yale, was brought in to sing the Commendatore. All the other roles were performed by students. I was Masetto. Busch directed it. The first time I ever heard the opera was one night at Mac's home, when he played a recording for me. It was from Glynbourne with Fritz Busch, Hans Busch's father, conducting.

Both Mac and Barbara took part in many productions themselves. They were both fine singers—Mac a dramatic baritone and Barbara a contralto. This past Saturday, listening to the Met broadcast of "*Cav*" and "*Pag*," I could not help but remember Mac's singing of Tonio in a production of those operas that we did in the summer of 1949. I sang the role of Silvio. I also remember Barbara's wonderful singing of the Old Maid in Menotti's *The Old Maid and the Thief*, with Mac singing the role of Bob (the Thief). The two of them even toured occasionally, doing the chamber opera, *The Secret of Suzanne*.

Mac was also an excellent German lieder singer and gave many marvelous recitals at Syracuse. He was also director of the choir at the university. After I graduated from Syracuse in 1950, I went to New York to try to begin a career, and there I worked with several other voice teachers. However, after a few years—despairing of finding someone with whom I could be satisfied, and missing Mac—I went back to studying with him, and continued with him until his death in 1988. He was teaching at the Boston Conservatory of Music at that time, as was Barbara.

Because of my long and close relationship with Mac, I spoke at his memorial service—and when I spoke of the great influence he had had on my life in so many ways, several of his former students came up to me after the service to say that he had had the same effect on them. Those of us who were fortunate enough to know him and to study with him found him to be a tough and demanding teacher, but a most inspiring one.

Happy memories!

David Fairchild, DMA, CMVT

Appendix C

Case Histories reported by David Blair McClosky

*W*e will now look at some interesting cases reported by McClosky.

Some years ago the National Association for Infantile Paralysis referred to me a young girl suffering from bulbar paralysis due to an attack of polio. This resulted in *bilateral paresis of the vocal folds* and constituted a constant danger to her health. Unable to cough up mucous or phlegm resulting from any respiratory infection, she had to have her lungs "pumped out" periodically to avoid chronic infection in respiratory areas below the larynx. My job was to teach her to cough somehow, thus overcoming the condition described.

What made my task doubly difficult was the fact that she had fallen into the habit of speaking with the intake of breath on inspiration—instead of with its expulsion. Gradually, through careful work to try to strengthen any muscles that could possibly be activated in her larynx, we were able to achieve the goal of getting her rid of phlegm. At the same time, she learned to speak on outgoing breath. So greatly did her voice and health improve that she was then able to resume her normal living and work.

A good many postoperative cases have been sent to me—patients who, because of a *laryngo-fissure* (removal of one vocal fold due to carcinoma of the larynx), had undergone serious loss of voice. Therapy has proved invaluable in these cases. Special attention is focused on exercises which cause the remaining fold to compensate by passing beyond the midline to make contact with the side of the larynx from which the other fold has been removed. A single vocal fold—which has been developed by therapy, vibrating with or against scar tissue—thus produces a voice far superior to the usual very husky postoperative voice.

Occupational vocal diseases occur in large numbers, and many speakers and singers come to me in search of relief. Teachers, ministers, priests, rabbis, auctioneers, lecturers, entertainers, politicians, salesmen—all those who use their voices more than usual, or more forcefully than usual—are subject to disorders of misuse, either because they do not know how to use their voices in the first place, or they do not know how to save their voices for important occasions.

You have probably known people who, when engaged in ordinary conversation, orated as if they were addressing a large audience. Not long ago, a teaching nun came to me with *chronic laryngitis*. She was somewhat over 40, and—although she enjoyed her work—was carrying a taxing schedule of classes for small children. Her voice had become thick and dark in color; her vocal folds were red, rough, and somewhat swollen. Formerly she had had a light high voice, she told me, but it had gradually become deep and coarse through the years as she had pushed it. She wanted very much to be able to go on with her teaching but was afraid that soon she would have no voice at all.

We worked together for several weeks and her voice gradually rose in pitch level. As the pressures were removed, and she learned how to relax the proper muscles in her throat, her voice became like that of a 13-year-old girl—high, light, and rather weak. To the other sisters, of course, this sounded unnatural; but as time went on her voice became stronger, fuller, and more mature-sounding at her correct pitch level. Finally, she came in to see me one day and—in answer to my "How are you today, sister?"—replied by singing in a clear, firm soprano that she was just fine. Her throat no longer became tired at the end of a long day, and she was able to chant during services as she had been able to do formerly. Her concentration and persistence in performing the exercises prescribed had effected this happy change.

About two years ago a middle-aged produce auctioneer was sent to me in great perturbation. He was forced to use his voice for hours on end every day; his livelihood depended upon its condition; and it had become almost unusable. *Vocal fold atrophy* had made it so husky that he could hardly make himself heard or understood. There was no fooling around on the part of this patient: he followed orders explicitly, meanwhile carrying on his business as usual. It took just six weeks to bring his folds back to normal and to give him back a clear, strong voice. Intermittent checkups since that time have shown the larynx to be healthy in every way.

Here was a case in which "the chips were down"—the patient's vocation was at stake, and there was no question in his mind as to the importance of the work we were doing together. It would be pleasant to report that all my patients were as conscientious as this man. Unfortunately, there are some who cannot see the value of any treatment unless it involves "taking shots" or swallowing pills at stated intervals. They seem to have no real understanding of what a functional disorder is, and they sit in my presence for several sessions expecting me to give them some miracle formula which will clear up their voice trouble overnight. They seem to expect me to do their exercises for them, like some of the weight-loss machines you see advertised. They remind me of the student who sits in the presence of a book for what he considers to be a sufficient length of time—not really concentrating upon its contents at all, but sure that somehow, possibly by osmosis, its ideas will magically infiltrate his mind and make him wise. Sometimes I have longed for a voice-therapy pill for these people.

And then sometimes—through some mysterious mental process—they suddenly see the light. Just as I am about to give them up as a bad job, they suddenly fathom what I am driving at and begin really to work at their exercises, finally realizing that they are the only ones who can actually cure themselves. It seems that they first have to be sold on what we are doing—perhaps by meeting another patient who has achieved a dramatic recovery, or perhaps through desperation, their doctor having told them that he can do nothing for them and that I am really their last resort.

Let me tell you of two quite similar cases—two men in executive positions in large corporations who came to me at about the same time with the same kind of throat ailments, and who well illustrate the difference between the patient who slights his exercises and the one who faithfully and systematically follows the regimen prescribed. Both men were high-powered business leaders; one was considerably older than the other and presumably more "set" in his ways. Strange to say, he was the more tractable—and it was the younger man, whom I shall call Mr. Y., and whom I shall first describe, who proved to be the "problem" patient.

Mr. Y. had an operation for the removal of polyps on his vocal folds and was warned by his doctor that his only chance of keeping a healthy voice was to go through a period of vocal retraining. This dynamic young man not only occupied a highly responsible position with his firm, but he also had the faculty and personality to head charity drives, organize alumni functions, and generally get himself into situations in which it was imperative for him to use his voice extensively. When he came to me, his voice was husky in the extreme and was used under constant strain. He was eager for relief—but unwilling to accept any discipline which would require time, a leisurely attitude, or the giving up of some of his many activities. His attitude, almost from the start, showed that he was highly skeptical of therapy—but that, since his doctor had ordered it, he might as well give it a try. Time after time his secretary would call me to break or postpone appointments; he had just been called into a conference, or out of town. A new appointment would be made, only to be postponed once more.

He was an engaging person to meet and talk with; a happily married family man, highly respected in any endeavor he undertook; and apparently suffered no psychological difficulties. But it did not take me long to realize that here was a patient almost impossible to control, a man unwilling to take the time or submit to the discipline required to give his voice a chance. In business he could delegate his routine jobs to others—and he couldn't understand why his therapy couldn't be similarly deputized. The last I heard of him was that he was about to go into the hospital for yet another operation on his larynx.

Now let me describe the case of the older man, Mr. Z. He had been under the care of several otolaryngologists. The year before he came to me, a small contact ulcer had developed on the middle surface of the posterior third of his right vocal fold, with inflammation surrounding it and also a slight inflammation of the opposite fold. He was put on voice rest at that time, but by March of the following year he again became hoarse and the ulceration reappeared in the region of the vocal process on the right arytenoid cartilage. He was fearful of throat cancer, but no malignancy was found, and rest was again prescribed. For three months the trouble seemed to be disappearing; but it started up again the following month. It was then that he came to me for treatment.

I worked with him for two months; then he returned to his doctor and was told that the ulcer had healed. The surface mucosa was almost intact and there was only a slight amount of granular tissue at the site of the healing ulcer. A month later he was completely cured—much to the satisfaction of his physician, who had written to me that he considered the case a difficult one indeed for voice therapy to improve. The patient went on with his business as usual. In six months he returned with a slight recurrence of his former trouble. He was somewhat husky and the folds were red. Happily he had remembered enough of our work together to need only two weeks of therapy to regain his vocal health. Since that time there has been no recurrence of the difficulty.

While Z. was undergoing treatment, and had begun to regain some normal use of his voice, he came in one day and told me how he saved his voice on an unusually trying day. He would instruct his secretary: "When I give you the high sign, tell the next person who has an appointment with me that I am having some difficulty with my voice and may not be able to talk at all." He then told of a meeting with a group of his business associates from out of town, which lasted several hours and had pretty well used up his voice. Later, they had some afterthoughts and asked to return for another conference. This was granted—but with the understanding that Mr. Z. would have to confine his remarks to writing. Following this "silent" discussion, my patient had enough voice left to finish out the day with needed conversation in a normal voice. This incident showed me to what lengths Z. was willing to go in complete cooperation with me and the prescribed therapy.

Therapy cases that were of purely psychological derivation puzzled me at first. My original thought was that such patients might be better off in the hands of a competent psychiatrist or psychotherapist. It did not take long, however, for me to discern that in many instances—whatever the psychological reason for the voice trouble—the cause had disappeared while still leaving the patient with a faulty pattern of phonation, and needing guidance in the proper ways of using the voice. Once such a pattern of muscular coordination has been established, it is difficult for it to be erased without training and considerable conscious thought.

In 1953 a man was sent to me with a case of *intermittent dysphonia* (hoarseness), which was seriously interfering with his responsible position in a large textile mill in northern New England. He had been troubled with this condition for more than six years. His larynx was normal in appearance, but when he began to speak his voice would squeeze off without warning into a high squeak, making him sound like an adolescent whose voice had not quite changed—or an oldster who has to make a great effort to get his folds to function. He had no idea what strange sound would issue next from his throat; even when he didn't squeak, his manner of speaking was forced and uncertain and made with great effort to push out some sort of sound which would not embarrass him.

Because many miles separated his home from my office, it was not possible for this patient to see me frequently, and accordingly, it took longer to correct this difficulty than would normally have been the case. After five months, however, his voice became clear, confident, and of fine quality, and it served him without fail, all day long in his taxing position. On one of his visits to Boston some time later, he telephoned and asked me if I knew who was speaking. For the life of me I could not tell. Imagine my astonishment when he told me—in firm, assured tones—that he was my ex-patient of the squeaky voice.

This case differed from most vocal abuse cases I have treated, in that his voice came down in pitch to a resonant baritone instead of going up from a croak to a normal, pleasing tone. In the elapsing years I have been gratified to find out that he has learned what to do when he feels the slightest vocal fatigue or tendency to return to his former mode of speaking. We had given special attention to exercises for relaxing the base of the tongue, the soft palate, and the hinge muscles of the jaw, in order to assure the smooth and unobstructed passage of breath through his nose and mouth. With this regimen, the patient has shown dramatic improvement.

Occasionally, coincidence enters into my work. Not long ago, two men came to me during the same year with the same, rather unusual pathology—a tendency toward *ventricular phonation*, coupled with thickened and reddened true vocal folds. Both of their voices were thick and husky, and low in pitch. One of them was a minister who had taken on an unconscionable amount of work in his parish. Aside from the weekly sermon ("Sunday is my easiest day," he told me), he had to use his voice constantly in counseling, comforting, speaking at luncheons, and talking incessantly to those thoughtless parishioners who telephoned him during mealtimes. He was a cheerful person who could not help being popular and in great demand. However, this very quality served him badly in that he was being taken advantage of, to the point where he was lucky to find a half-hour during the week for meditation or relaxation with his family.

The other patient was a social-service director; again, I found him an extraordinarily pleasant and likeable person. He loved to talk, and his work involved speaking to groups and interviewing people all day. But he found that as the day wore on his voice would begin to leave him, and—with several interviews yet to come—he would have to push his voice until it finally became a whisper.

Now, I do not often prescribe whispering—it is not particularly healthful and under some conditions may even be harmful. However, I asked both of these patients to whisper for a few days—in the softest and most relaxed manner possible—until they had acquired some slight knowledge of what I wanted them to do with their voices. Then they began to use a soft, breathy manner of phonation, and from there we progressed to the usual treatment for such cases.

Both of these men had the same incentive—indeed, the same necessity—to regain their vocal health, and both worked equally hard to do it. In approximately one month of concentrated effort each had regained his healthy voice and pitch level. Instead of the coarse, low, croaky voices that they had used in the beginning to describe their difficulty, they turned out to possess voices of excellent tenor quality. Both have long since returned to their respective fields of endeavor and have written me several times to report that their voices remain in a fine and healthy condition—even showing further development along the right lines, as should be the case. Mutual friends also have reported that they "sound fine."

Many people feel that, with advancing age, their voices will naturally deteriorate—as do so many of our other bodily functions. They expect to fit naturally into the "sixth age" described by Jacques in Shakespeare's *As You Like It*: ". . . and his big manly voice/ Turning again toward childish treble, pipes/ And whistles in his sound." As a third and final example of parallel cases described in this appendix, let me tell you about two older men who came to me a few years ago. I cite these cases to prove that old age does not necessarily mean deterioration of the voice.

The first gentleman was sent to me for voice therapy during his three-week summer vacation. He was then 79. For more than 40 years, he had been Speaker of the Senate in his Midwestern state and was still an active trial lawyer. When I first saw him, his voice was only a bare whisper from *vocal fold atrophy*. We worked together twice a day for only 15 days—and by that time his voice had returned to a strong, rich bass, which he was using without effort. He returned home and I did not see him for another six months. He told me then that when he went back to work, one of his colleagues said that his voice sounded as it had 40 years before! Six years later, when he was 85 (and *still* practicing law), he wrote to me, "My voice is as good as ever."

The other man was 65 when I first saw him, and he came to me not for voice therapy, but for singing lessons! He had sung all his life and had been a successful tenor—confining his singing career, however, to church work and singing for various community groups, since he also was a busy lawyer and politician. He told me that he had not been able to sing well for the past 15 years and had completely lost his upper tenor range. In fact, he became so discouraged with his voice that he had given up all professional singing some time before. He wanted to know if I could do anything with the voice of a man his age. I assured him that I could help him, and we worked together for a year and a half. His voice became stronger and stronger and soon regained its former range. I remarked at one of his lessons, "It seems to me that your voice now must be in as good shape as it was years ago." His answer was, "On the contrary. Let's face it, I was never able to use it so easily before!"

In summary, we are fortunate that there are now medical or therapeutic treatments for all voice disorders, as well as a number of excellent centers across the United States that are dedicated to voice problems. While surgical intervention may seem the quickest solution for an individual suffering from a voice disorder, caution is advisable—especially for singers. The delicate adjustments necessary for the refined tasks of singing require not only excellent muscular coordination but also excellent condition of the vibratory edge of the vocal fold and the somewhat gelatinous layer beneath it. The primary danger of surgery is scarring, which—despite some fascinating research—at this writing remains irreversible. Surgery should, therefore, be considered a last resort.

Voice therapy should be a part of treatment for most voice disorders, since the functional component should be addressed as well as any underlying medical cause. Further, there is a need to define what is "normal," so that medical insurance will cover therapy to recover "normal" function. In the case of professional voice users, many of them need to function much better than current definitions of "normal," and insurance may not provide adequate coverage to achieve this. Lastly, there remains a need for cross-training and better communication between otolaryngologists, speech pathologists, and singing teachers, so that they may work most effectively together for the benefit of the patient.

Appendix D

The McClosky Institute of Voice

The McClosky Institute of Voice Inc. was founded in 1979 and incorporated in 1981 on the belief that David Blair McClosky's pioneering work in the field of voice and vocal rehabilitation must continue to grow and flourish. Mr. McClosky was a pioneer in the field of vocal rehabilitation in the 1950s, and many of his students became loyal, dedicated teachers of the McClosky Technique. Lin Wallin Schuller, who worked closely with McClosky, had the inspiration and dedication to make the Institute a reality. In January 1981, the organization was incorporated, and the bylaws of the Institute were ratified. This nonprofit organization is dedicated to the maintenance and enhancement of healthy voices, as well as offering care and help for troubled voices.

In its formative years, the organization provided ongoing education for its own members, who were teachers, speech pathologists, and performers. In 1982, the Institute held its first seminar for others interested in voice and vocal health: music educators, choral conductors, speech and language pathologists, public speakers, and singers. Its professional development programs consist of seminars and workshops offered in the United States and abroad on an ongoing basis.

In 1996, the McClosky Institute of Voice began a Certification Program (Certified McClosky Voice Technician—CMVT), under which qualified people are trained to teach the McClosky Technique. Developed by Dr. Bonnie Pomfret and Janet Alcorn, the course consists of 120 hours of instruction and practicum over two summers. It is taught by Master Teachers, and continues to increase the number of people who are able to provide this valuable technique to the public.

The stated purposes of the Institute are:

- The furtherance and propagation of the vocal technique of David Blair McClosky through training of voice technicians therein
- The creation of a nationwide association of qualified voice technicians
- The selection and designation of certain qualified voice technicians as Certified McClosky Voice Technicians
- The establishment of a liaison between qualified voice technicians and the medical profession
- Research into the broader applications of McClosky Vocal Techniques.

Following is a partial list of institutions where CMVTs have taught or lectured on the McClosky Technique.

- Academy of Music, Vienna, Austria
- Birmingham Southern College, Birmingham, AL
- Bob Jones University, Greenville, SC
- Boston Conservatory of Music, Boston, MA
- Boston University, Boston, MA
- Bradford College, Haverhill, MA
- Brenau University, Gainesville, GA
- Bridgewater State College, Bridgewater, MA
- Calvin College, Grand Rapids, MI
- Central University for Nationalities, Beijing, China
- Cleveland Institute of Music, Cleveland, OH
- Cornell University, Ithaca, NY
- Duke University, Durham, NC
- East Texas Baptist University, Marshall, TX
- Eastman School of Music, Rochester, NY
- Emmanuel College, Boston, MA
- Emory Voice Center, Atlanta, GA
- Five Towns College, Dix Hills, LI, NY
- Furman University, Greenville, SC
- Georgia Perimeter College, Atlanta, GA
- Glinka Choir College, St. Petersburg, Russia
- Guilford College, Greensboro, NC

- Hartnell College, Salinas, CA
- Hartt School of Music, West Hartford, CT
- Harvard University, Cambridge MA
- Hunter College, New York, NY
- Illinois State University, Normal, IL
- Indiana University, Bloomington, IN
- Iowa Central Community College, Fort Dodge, IA
- Iowa State University, Ames, IA
- Kalamazoo College, Kalamazoo, MI
- Mannes College of Music, New York, NY
- Marquette University, Milwaukee, WI
- Marygrove College, Detroit, MI
- Massachusetts College of Art, Boston, MA
- Massachusetts Eye and Ear Infirmary, Boston, MA
- Meredith College, Raleigh, NC
- Methodist Theological School, Sibu, Sarawak, Malaysia
- Nanyang Technological University, Singapore
- New England Conservatory of Music, Boston, MA
- New York College of Medicine at Syracuse
- New York Singing Teachers' Association, New York, NY
- North Carolina School of the Arts, Winston-Salem, NC
- Northwest Louisiana State University, Natchitoches, LA
- Oakland University, Rochester, MI
- Queens College, New York, NY
- Queens College, Charlotte, NC
- Rhode Island College, Providence, RI
- Roger Williams University, Bristol, RI
- Salve Regina University, Newport, RI
- St. Elizabeth's Hospital, Boston, MA
- St. Mary's College, Terre Haute, IN
- San José State University, San José, CA
- Seattle University, Seattle WA
- Seattle Pacific University, Seattle, WA
- Shorter College, Rome, GA
- Silliman University, Dumaguete City, Philippines
- Simmons College, Boston, MA

- Skidmore College, Saratoga Springs, NY
- Smith College, Northampton, MA
- Southern Illinois University, Carbondale, IL
- State University of New York, Buffalo, NY
- Syracuse University, Syracuse, NY
- Texas Christian University, Fort Worth, TX
- University of Alabama, Birmingham, AL
- University of Bremen, Bremen, Germany
- University of California, Santa Cruz, CA
- University of Lowell, Lowell, MA
- University of Michigan, Ann Arbor, MI
- University of Minnesota, Minneapolis, MN
- University of North Carolina, Chapel Hill, NC
- University of North Carolina, Greensboro, NC
- University of the Philippines, Quezon City, Philippines
- Vassar College, Poughkeepsie, NY
- Voice Evaluation Clinic, Peoria ENT Associates, Peoria, IL
- Voice Foundation International Symposium, Philadelphia, PA
- Washington University, St. Louis, MO
- Wellesley College, Wellesley, MA
- Western Michigan University, Kalamazoo, MI
- Westfield State College, Westfield, MA

Appendix E

Certification in the McClosky Technique

$\mathcal{T}$he McClosky Institute of Voice sponsors workshops and courses, generally held during the summer months, at various locations around the United States. These courses are taught by Certified McClosky Voice Technicians (CMVTs), who have been thoroughly trained in the application and teaching of McClosky's techniques, as well as related areas of anatomy, physiology, and voice disorders. Originally, all CMVTs were taught in specialized courses at Boston University or Boston Conservatory, by McClosky himself, with practicum experience taking place at the Massachusetts Eye and Ear Infirmary's Voice Therapy Clinic.

In 1996, the Institute initiated the training of Certified McClosky Voice Technicians in a two-summer course. The 120-hour course consists of a scientific component (anatomy, physiology, and voice disorders), an applied component (McClosky Technique and its applications), and a pedagogical component (observation of CMVTs and supervised teaching). In addition to the academic requirements of the course, CMVTs are required not only to demonstrate knowledge of the techniques but also to exemplify good voice use in their own teaching and singing.

In 2008, 50 CMVTs were practicing in 19 states, Canada, the Philippines, and Singapore. The Institute maintains a website with a directory of its certified instructors (http://www.mcclosky.org). This directory includes only certified instructors, and not the thousands of others who have trained with McClosky or CMVTs, and are currently active as singers, teachers, choral conductors, speech pathologists, actors, and politicians.

Appendix D contains a listing of educational institutions where CMVTs teach or have taught.

McClosky and the Voice Team

The McClosky Institute trains its CMVTs to understand and guide basic voice production. The technique is simple, gentle, methodical, and especially effective in dealing with muscle tension. It can be used to enhance a healthy voice, to develop an untrained voice, and to provide a solid basis for phonation in a disabled voice. Mr. McClosky trained singers, actors, teachers, choral conductors, speech pathologists, salespeople, politicians, members of the clergy, and attorneys. The Institute's certification courses were designed to conform to the recommendations for cross-training of voice teachers by the Joint NATS/ASHA Committee (1992).

- Ethics, professionalism, and privacy issues are part of the certification curriculum described above. McClosky CMVTs are expected to adhere to the highest standards of professionalism and ethics.

- CMVTs have served as referral voice specialists for several medical voice centers and teams, including Henry Ford Hospital (Detroit, MI), Emory Voice Center (Atlanta, GA), Evelyn Trammell Voice & Swallowing Center (Atlanta, GA), Massachusetts Eye and Ear Infirmary (Boston, MA), Boston Medical Center (Boston, MA), Peoria Ear Nose and Throat Group (Peoria, IL), Brigham and Women's Hospital, (Boston, MA), and Grabscheid Voice Center at Mt. Sinai Hospital (New York, NY).

Appendix F

Contributors

Janet Alcorn, CMVT and Master Teacher, earned her BM degree from Northwestern University, and a MM in Voice and Voice Therapy from Boston University. She was a member of the Metropolitan Opera Studio and New York City Opera, and has sung major roles with the opera companies of Cleveland, Dallas, Philadelphia, Frankfurt, and Manila and as soloist with many symphony orchestras including Philadelphia, Cleveland, and Cincinnati. She has also studied extensively in the Alexander Technique and Body Mapping. She is a certified Andover Educator. She has taught at the Cleveland Institute of Music, Hartt School of Music, Birmingham Southern College, and is Associate Professor Emerita at Iowa State University.

Maria Argyros, CMVT and Master Teacher, received a BS degree from the Crane School of Music, SUNY, Potsdam, and an MS degree from Emerson College, Boston, with post-graduate study at Peabody Conservatory, NYU, Westminster Choir College, and Illinois State University. She was a student of Mr. McClosky. Ms. Argyros has been a referral voice teacher for the Grabscheid Voice Center at Mt. Sinai Hospital in New York. She maintains a private voice studio in Manhattan and is a visiting Associate Professor of Voice at Hunter College in Manhattan and The Aaron Copland School of Music, Queens College, where she teaches applied voice, voice classes, and vocal pedagogy. As a performer, she has sung over 20 major opera roles and has appeared as soloist in oratorio in New York's Alice Tully Hall, St. Thomas Church, and throughout the Northeast.

Eric R. Bronner, CMVT, tenor, holds a BA from Purdue University, an MS from Ohio University, and an MM from Longy School of Music. He is a faculty member at Roger Williams University and Salve Regina University (RI). He specializes in uniting McClosky techniques with Contemporary Com-

103

mercial Music Vocal Pedagogy, having also certified in LoVetri Somatic Voice Work.™ He has performed with the Aldeburgh Fringe Music Festival (UK), the Napa Zarzuela Festival (CA), First Coast Opera (FL), Townsend Opera (CA), American Classics (MA), Opera Providence (RI), and has aired on BBC, NPR, and PBS media. He has authored three articles in the *NATS Journal of Singing*.

David Fairchild, CMVT, holds the BA and BM from Syracuse University, where he was a student of David Blair McClosky, and an MM and DMA from Columbia University Teachers College. Dr. Fairchild taught vocal music in the Eastchester Junior and Senior High Schools, and voice and piano privately with studios in New York City and Westchester County. As a baritone soloist, he has sung at Christ Church in Bronxville, New York, and has toured the U.S. and Canada.

Jay D. Lane, CMVT, holds a PhD in musicology from Yale University. Lane is a voice teacher, tenor, conductor, and organist, and has conducted for the Yale Bach Society and the Yale Gilbert and Sullivan Society. He conducts the Wakefield Choral Society and leads Vox Lucens, a 12-voice Renaissance choir, in which he also sings first tenor. He teaches voice privately in Acton, Massachusetts, and serves as organist and choir director at the Church of the Good Shepherd.

Bonnie Pomfret, CMVT and Master Teacher, holds the DM in voice from Indiana University, the MM in Voice from Boston Conservatory (where she was a student of David Blair McClosky), and the SMP degree in voice and piano from the Musikhochschule Freiburg, Germany. She has sung as a soprano soloist in recital, oratorio, and chamber music in the U.S., Asia, and Europe. She has served as a singing voice specialist at Emory Voice Center and Peoria (IL) ENT Group. Pomfret has taught at Boston University, Illinois State University, Emory University, Shorter College, the University of Alabama at Birmingham, Salve Regina University, and Boston University.

Lin Wallin Schuller, CMVT and Master Teacher, trained with David Blair McClosky at Boston University and completed the graduate course in Voice Therapy at the Boston Conservatory of Music. Schuller has lectured throughout the United States on children's voice development, the aging voice, and voice technique for music educators, voice teachers, speech pathologists, singers, speakers, and storytellers. She maintains a private studio in Easton, MA, and has directed a number of church choirs in Massachusetts. She served as the Supervisor of the Voice Therapy Clinic at the Massachusetts Eye and Ear Infirmary in Boston for seven years and is the Founding President of the McClosky Institute of Voice.